From the Guidance of

Surah YaSeen

Author by
Umm Muhammad

Introduction

A Makkan *sūrah*[1] of eighty-three *āyahs,*[2] *Yā Seen* is named after the two opening letters of the *sūrah. Sūrah* names are not an integral part of the Qur'ān, and most of them were not designated by the Prophet ﷺ. Often it happened that a distinguishing word in a particular *sūrah* or a word defining a *sūrah's* subject matter became a common means of identification among the *ṣaḥābah* and later scholars. In fact, some *sūrahs* were known by several such key words. Even today, with the tendency toward standardization, a few *sūrahs* are listed in *muṣ·ḥafs* under alternative titles.[3]

The subjects treated in this *sūrah* are those most generally found in Makkan revelation – namely, *tawḥeed,* the resurrection and Hereafter, and the prophethood of Muḥammad ﷺ. Its object being to establish a firm foundation of faith, *YāSeen* presents arguments appealing to reason and brings to witness some of the visible signs of the unlimited power and ability of Allāh (ﷻ). Its quick and almost choppy rhythm seems to knock repeatedly against the senses, adding to the effect of the varied scenes which are presented one after another throughout the *sūrah.* Evidence is clear. Warnings are forceful and severe. Only a heart which deliberately rejects and refuses the truth can remain unmoved.

Several *ḥadīths* are often quoted in connection with *Sūrah Yā Seen.* Although none are classified as ṣaḥeeḥ, perhaps the most accepted among them is that narrated by Aḥmad, Abū Dāwūd, an-Nasā'ī and Ibn Mājah in which Ma'qil bin Yasār reported that the Messenger of Allāh ﷺ said, اقرؤوها على موتاكم "Recite it over your dying ones," meaning *Yā Seen.*[4] In Arabic, the word "*mawtā*" is used according to specific contexts to mean either "dying" or "dead." The first meaning in this case is supported by another *ḥadīth* which uses the same word: لقنوا موتاكم لا إله إلا الله "Help your dying ones to say, '*Lā ilāha ill-Allāh.*'"[5] Obviously, this could not apply to the dead but only to those on the verge of death.

Imām Aḥmad mentioned that the scholars used to say, "When *YāSeen* is read for the dying, Allāh eases it for him by that." By this he meant that Allāh makes the exit of the soul easier, just as recitation of the *sūrah* is said to ease any difficult matter. He also reported in his Musnad from Ṣafwān: "My shaykhs told me that they were with Ghudhayf bin al-Ḥārith ath-Thumāli when he was dying. He said, 'Can any of you recite

---

The word "sūrah," meaning a chapter of the Qur'ān, is derived from "sūr" or "wall" in Arabic. It literally means "something enclosed or contained – a separate entity."

Although the specific meaning of "āyah" is "verse" when referring to the Qur'ān, its general meaning is "sign." Each verse of the Qur'ān is a sign from Allāh.

For example, Sūrah at-Tawbah is also called Barā'ah, Sūrah Ghāfir is called al-Mu'min, Sūrah Fuṣṣilat is Ḥā Meem as-Sajdah, Sūrah al-Insān is ad-Dahr, Sūrah al-'Alaq is Iqra', and Sūrah al-Masad is al-Lahab.

4Although considered ṣaḥeeḥ by al-Ḥākim and Ibn Ḥibbān, the contemporary muḥaddith, Shaykh Nāṣir ud-Deen al-Albānī, has pointed out weakness in this tradition. Other scholars, however, have considered it sufficient to establish a sunnah.

Muslim, Abū Dāwūd and at-Tirmidhī.

Yā-Seen?' So Ṣāliḥ bin Shurayḥ as-Sakūni recited it, and when he reached the fortieth ayah, Ghudhayf passed away. My shaykhs used to say that when it is recited in the presence of one who is dying, it eases the pain of death." That was the opinion of Ṣafwān. 'Eesā bin al-Mu'tamir recited it for Ibn Ma'bad [when he was dying].[6]

Some, however, have mistakenly taken the word "*mawtākum*" in the *ḥadīth* of Ma'qil bin Yasār to mean "your dead," thus assuming that the *sūrah* is to be read in ceremonies after death. Therefore, one should be reminded that aside from the usual procedures of washing, shrouding, funeral prayer and burial, there are no further "ceremonies." Imām ash-Shāfi'ī, Imām Aḥmad and many other scholars deplored the practice of special gatherings being held (even during the usual condolence period), as this is contrary to the *sunnah* and prevents the family from returning to normal life as soon as possible, prolonging their pain and sadness.[7] What can be said, then, of the many un-Islamic innovations practiced by later generations for which preparations are made, time and money are wasted, and which consist of outright disobedience – often being renewed on the seventh day, the fortieth day, the first anniversary and sometimes beyond?!

When Ja'far bin Abī Ṭālib was killed, the Prophet ﷺ said, "Prepare food for the family of Ja'far, for something has happened which has distracted them."[8] Yet, today we find that in addition to their affliction, the family of the deceased is expected to provide food for guests, who are often a burden upon them, sometimes going into debt to do so or spending from that which rightfully belongs to orphans or others in need. One seriously wonders when Muslims will begin to fear Allāh and discard these sinful customs.

Even the practice of gathering after a death with the intent of completing the recitation of certain parts or all of the Qur'ān is an innovation in religion which cannot, therefore, be praiseworthy. It was not done by the Prophet ﷺ, his companions or any of their faithful followers. The Qur'ān was revealed by Allāh for the benefit of the living. Indeed, there is no doubt that reading or recitation at any time benefits the reader and would also be comforting to the family of the deceased. What is objectionable, however, is the stipulation of certain conditions as to when and how it must be done, turning it into a ritual. Many scholars are of the opinion that the reward for recitation does not reach the dead in any case. Thus, one should concentrate instead on supplication for the deceased or charity on his behalf, about which there is no doubt and which is encouraged in the *sunnah.* May Allāh guide us and cover us with His mercy both in life and in death.

---

[6] Narrated by Aḥmad. Shaykh al-Albāni said in *Irwā' al-Ghaleel*, 3/152: "This is a ṣaḥeeḥ sanad going back to Ghudhayf bin al-Ḥārith, may Allah be pleased with him. Its men are thiqāt apart from 'the shaykhs' who are not named and are therefore unknown (majhūl). But the fact that they are unknown is compensated for by their large number, especially since they are of the generation of the Tābi'een..."

[7] Rather, in relation to condolences, the sunnah is that aside from those who are present for the purpose of assisting, guests should enter, give comfort to the family and stay only briefly without lingering.

[8] Abū Dāwūd and at-Tirmidhī – *ṣaḥeeḥ.*

بسم الله الرحمن الرحيم

Section One – Āyahs 1-12

يس (١) وَالقُرآنِ الحَكِيمِ (٢) إِنَّكَ لَمِنَ المُرسَلِينَ (٣) عَلَى صِرَاطٍ مُستَقِيمٍ (٤) تَنزِيلَ العَزِيزِ الرَّحِيمِ
(٥) لِتُنذِرَ قَومًا مَا أُنذِرَ آبَاؤُهُم فَهُم غَافِلُونَ (٦) لَقَدْ حَقَّ القَولُ عَلَى أَكثَرِهِم فَهُم لايُؤمِنُونَ (٧) إِنَّا جَعَلنَا
فِي أَعنَاقِهِم أَغلالاً فَهِيَ إِلَى الأَذقَانِ فَهُم مُقمَحُونَ (٨) وَجَعَلنَا مِن بَينِ أَيدِيهِم سَدًّا وَمِن خَلفِهِم سَدًّا
فَأَغشَينَاهُم فَهُم لايُبصِرُونَ (٩) وَسَوَاءٌ عَلَيهِم أَأَنذَرتَهُم أَم لَم تُنذِرهُم لايُؤمِنُونَ (١٠) إِنَّمَا تُنذِرُ مَنِ اتَّبَعَ
الذِّكرَ وَخَشِيَ الرَّحمنَ بِالغَيبِ فَبَشِّرْهُ بِمَغفِرَةٍ وَأَجرٍ كَرِيمٍ (١١) إِنَّا نَحنُ نُحيِي المَوتَى وَنَكتُبُ مَا قَدَّمُوا
وَآثَارَهُم وَكُلَّ شَيءٍ أَحصَينَاهُ فِي إِمَامٍ مُبِينٍ (١٢)

(1) Yā Seen (2) By the wise Qur'ān (3) Certainly you are from among the messengers (4) On a straight path (5) A revelation of the Mighty, the Merciful (6) That you may warn a people whose forefathers were not warned, so they are unaware. (7) Already the Word has come into effect upon most of them, so they do not believe. (8) Indeed, We have put shackles around their necks, which are up to their chins, so their heads are kept aloft. (9) And We have put before them a barrier and behind them a barrier and covered them so they do not see. (10) And it is all the same to them whether you warn them or do not warn them they will not believe. (11) You can only warn one who follows the Remembrance and fears ar-Raḥmān unseen. So give him good tidings of forgiveness and of generous reward. (12) It is We who bring the dead to life and record what they have put forth and left behind, and all things We have enumerated in a clear register.

بسم الله الرحمن الرحيم

In the name of Allāh, the Entirely and Especially Merciful

The phrase "*Bismillāh*" has been explained by students of grammar as being an abbreviation, its complete meaning understood in context as: "I begin in the name of Allāh." Ibn ‘Abbās stated that the Messenger of Allāh ﷺ would not know where a *sūrah* ended and the next one began until the revelation to him of the words "*Bismillāh ir-Raḥmān ir-Raḥeem.*"[9]

Ar-Raḥmān ar-Raḥeem are two of Allāh's descriptive names derived from the word "*raḥmah*" (mercy), both being intensive forms of "merciful" (i.e., extremely merciful). A double meaning is intended by using both together.

---

[9]Abū Dāwūd - *ṣaḥeeḥ*.

Raḥmān is used only to describe Allāh, while *raḥeem* might be used to describe a person as well. The Prophet ﷺ was described in the Qur'ān as "*raḥeem.*" *Raḥmān* is above and beyond the human capacity – intensely merciful. Lest intensity be understood as something of limited duration, Allāh describes Himself further as *Raḥeem* – continually merciful.

Raḥmān also carries a wider and more general meaning – merciful to all creation. Justice is a part of this mercy. *Raḥeem* has a meaning of specificity – especially and specifically merciful to the believers. Forgiveness is a part of this mercy.[10]

Āyah 1

Yā Seen يس

These two letters, from which the *sūrah* takes its name, are among the fourteen which occur in various combinations at the beginning of twenty-nine *sūrahs* in the Qur'ān. There has been much speculation as to the meanings of these opening letters, but, in reality, they belong to that category of *āyahs* about which true knowledge rests only with Allāh. Since this is the case, some scholars have maintained that it is not permissible to try to explain them in any way. Others have submitted that they are among the proofs given by Allāh (*subḥānahu wa ta'ālā*) of the inimitability of the Qur'ān since He has kept their purpose to Himself. They have noted that almost always the opening letters are followed by a reference to the Qur'ān or the Book – as if a challenge to all humanity, which stands helpless to oppose divine scripture by producing anything similar to it. Human failure remains, in spite of the fact that this Book consists of the same phonetic symbols used by men who pride themselves on linguistic skill. Any assertion beyond this point as to actual meanings must be rejected as having no basis in the Qur'ān or the *sunnah* of the Prophet ﷺ.

Concerning this *āyah* in particular, it has been stated that "*Yā Seen*" is a name designated to Allāh's Messenger ﷺ because the third *āyah* (following an oath) addresses him directly. Other theories hold that the letters represent a name of Allāh or carry the meaning: "O mankind" (*yā insān*). Again there is no proof for any of these statements, and one can only attribute certain knowledge to their author, Allāh, the Exalted.

[10]See al-Qurṭubī's *al-Jāmi'u li Aḥkām il-Qur'ān,* pp. 103-107.

Āyah 2

By the wise Qur'ān وَالقُرْآنِ الحَكِيمِ

Allāh (*subḥānahu wa ta'ālā*) swears by the Qur'ān, full of wisdom. The letter "*wāw*" (و), which translates here as "by," is understood to stand for the phrase "I swear by" and designates an oath. While it is unacceptable that a man should take an oath except in the name of Allāh,[11] He (ﷻ) may swear by whatever He wills, be it Himself, His creations, His signs or His revelation.

An oath is a means of confirmation or removing doubt from the mind. The Qur'ān was revealed to all people, among them those who accept truth readily, those who doubt and hesitate, and those who deny. The oath, when used by Allāh (ﷻ), serves to erase all doubts, clarify any questions, establish evidence and confirm information absolutely.

The Qur'ān is described as "*ḥakeem*" (wise), and this is an adjective normally used for an intelligent being. Thus, the words of Allāh are characterized with the qualities of life, will, purpose and discrimination, which are essential to wisdom. "*Ḥakeem*" also carries the meaning of having been made precise or exact – that which neither contains any fault or contradiction nor is subject to change. The Qur'ān speaks with the perfect knowledge of the Creator about His creation. It teaches with wisdom and establishes the best system of life for humanity.

One is immediately alerted by an oath from Allāh (ﷻ) that a most important statement is to follow – the object of His concern...

Āyah 3

Certainly you are from among the messengers إِنَّكَ لَمِنَ المُرسَلِينَ

Allāh (*subḥānahu wa ta'ālā*) swears in order to remove any and all misgivings about the prophethood of Muḥammad ﷺ, stating categorically and directly to him: ***"Certainly you, [O Muḥammad], are from among the messengers."***[12] The statement assumes the acceptance by the people of the fact that previous messengers were sent by Allāh to mankind, and it goes on to confirm that Muḥammad ﷺ is surely one of them. This essential point of faith is one of the main subjects of Makkan *sūrahs* and is picked up again near the end of this *sūrah* in *āyah* 69. Sayyid Quṭb has drawn attention to the fact that in the present *āyah,* Allāh (*subḥānahu wa ta'ālā*) addresses His prophet directly

[11] 'Umar bin al-Khaṭṭāb reported that the Messenger of Allāh (ﷺ) said, "Whoever swears by other than Allāh has disbelieved or committed *shirk* [association with Him]." At-Tirmidhī considered it *ḥasan*; al-Ḥākim graded it *ṣaḥeeḥ*.

[12] The word "*mursal*" (singular of *mursaleen*) literally means "one who is sent." "*Rasūl*" is also used for "messenger."

rather than the people, showing that the subject of his prophethood is a truth not to be discussed or argued with them. Rather, it is established and confirmed by Him, irrespective of their opinions.

Ibn 'Abbās related that the disbelievers of Quraysh confronted the Prophet ﷺ, saying, "You are not, O Muḥammad, a messenger, and Allāh has not sent you to us." In this verse Allāh (*subḥānahu wa ta'ālā*) refutes this statement, swearing by the great and precise Qur'ān that Muḥammad ﷺ was indeed from the messengers.[13]

Āyah 4

On a straight path عَلَى صِرَاطٍ مُستَقِيمٍ

On a straight and direct path, which is defined by Allāh and explained by all of His messengers – the way of submission to His will:

صِرَاطِ اللهِ الَّذِي لَهُ مَا فِي السَّمَاوَاتِ وَمَا فِي الأَرضِ

"The path of Allāh to whom belongs the heavens and earth..."[14]

Aṣ-ṣirāṭ al-mustaqeem (the straight path) is further explained in *Sūrah al-Fātiḥah* as:

صِرَاطَ الَّذِينَ أَنعَمتَ عَلَيهِم غَيرِ المَغضُوبِ عَلَيهِم وَلا الضَّالِّينَ ***"The way of those whom You have blessed, not of those who have evoked [Your] anger nor of those who have gone astray."***[15]

The nature of this message brought by all prophets is uprightness and straightforwardness. Its truth is clear with no obscurity and no supposition, bending neither with human whims nor with temporary worldly interests – direct, uncomplicated and in harmony with the nature of man and his surroundings.

In describing the "straight path," various commentators have designated its meanings as Islām, the *sunnah* of the Prophet ﷺ, following the Book of Allāh, the path of worship, obedience to Allāh, and acting in accordance with the Qur'ān and the *sunnah*. All of these are essentially the same and are correct.[16]

---

[13]Recorded by al-Qurṭubī in his *tafseer*.
[14]Sūrah ash-Shūrā, 42:53.
[15]Sūrah al-Fātiḥah, 1:7.
[16]Fatāwā Ibn Taymiyyah.

Āyah 5

A revelation of the Mighty, the Merciful تَنزِيلَ الْعَزِيزِ الرَّحِيمِ

This revelation,[17] the Qur'ān, is the guide for those who seek to follow the Straight Path. It has been sent down to mankind by al-'Azeez, the One who has power over all things and could certainly have forced all men to submit to His will in Islam if He had so chosen. And yet, He is also ar-Raḥeem, especially merciful (beyond His general mercy to all creatures) to those who believe in Him and who follow His guidance.

Āyah 6

لِتُنذِرَ قَوْمًا مَا أُنذِرَ آبَاؤُهُمْ فَهُمْ غَافِلُونَ

That you may warn a people whose forefathers were not warned, so they are unaware

Muḥammad bin 'Abdullāh ﷺ was raised among a people who had known no other prophet since the time of Ismā'eel (upon him be peace). Although they had not completely forgotten Allāh, the Arabs worshipped Him superficially, usually associating manmade deities with Him, calling upon them in supplication and obeying only the law of their own desires and corrupted customs.

Although Prophet Muḥammad ﷺ was sent to the whole of mankind, he naturally had to begin his invitation to Allāh with his own people and initially within his own family. Ibn 'Abbās related that when Allāh (ﷻ) revealed the āyah: وَأَنذِرْ عَشِيرَتَكَ الأَقْرَبِينَ ***"And warn your nearest kinsmen,"***[18] the Prophet ﷺ mounted aṣ-Ṣafā, calling out to assemble the people, and then said to them, "Would you believe me if I informed you that [enemy] horses were atop the mountain waiting to attack?" "Yes," they replied. He said, "Then believe that I am a warner to you of a severe punishment to come!" At that, his uncle, Abū Lahab, snapped, "Is it for this that you have gathered us?! May you have loss and destruction all day long." At that, Allāh revealed: تَبَّتْ يَدَا أَبِي لَهَبٍ وَتَبَّ "May the hands of Abū Lahab be destroyed, and destroyed is he..." to the end of Sūrah al-Masad.[19]

---

[17]The word "*tanzeel,*" literally, "a sending down," is derived from "*nazzala,*" meaning "to let down bit by bit." This is opposed to "*anzala,*" which means "to let down all at once."
[18]Sūrah ash-Shu'arā', 26:214.
[19]Al-Bukhārī, Muslim, at-Tirmidhī and an-Nasā'ī. The Qur'ānic reference is *Sūrah al-Masad,* 111:1.

Additionally, when the aforementioned āyah (26:214) was revealed, 'Ā'ishah reported that the Prophet ﷺ arose and said, "O Fāṭimah, daughter of Muḥammad! O Ṣafiyyah, daughter of 'Abdul-Muṭṭalib! O sons of 'Abdul-Muṭṭalib! I cannot avail you before Allāh at all, but you can ask me of my property what you wish."[20] And Abū Hurayrah reported that he ﷺ called out, "O people of Quraysh, save yourselves from the Fire! O people of Banī Ka'b, save yourselves from the Fire! O people of Banī Hāshim, save yourselves from the Fire! O people of 'Abdul-Muṭṭalib, save yourselves from the Fire! O Fāṭimah, daughter of Muḥammad, save yourself from the Fire!"[21]

There is no doubt that the message of Islam was never meant to be limited to the Arabs. The Prophet ﷺ made it clear that he was sent to all mankind – black and white, Arab and non-Arab. He sent messages of warning and invitation to Islam to the rulers of neighboring nations and empires. In the Qur'ān, Allāh ordered him to say:

قُلْ يَا أَيُّهَا النَّاسُ إِنِّي رَسُولُ اللهِ إِلَيكُم جَمِيعًا

"O people, truly I am the messenger of Allāh to all of you..."[22]

Furthermore, He (ﷻ) stated: وَمَا أَرسَلنَاكَ إِلاَّ كَافَّةً لِلنَّاسِ بَشِيرًا وَنَذِيرًا

"And We have not sent you except inclusively to all the people as a giver of good tidings and a warner..."[23]

Unawareness (ghaflah) is a serious ailment of the heart, blocking its natural function of reception and response to truth and righteousness. It often takes a shock of some sort to initiate an awakening, and an appropriate treatment for a people unaware of the consequences of their behavior is a warning that they are in danger.

Āyah 7

لَقَدْ حَقَّ القَولُ عَلَى أَكثَرِهِم فَهُم لايُؤمِنُونَ

Already the Word has come into effect upon most of them, so they do not believe.

"The Word" here refers to the decree of Allāh (ﷻ) – very likely the same that is mentioned in *Sūrah as-Sajdah*: ...لأَملأَنَّ جَهَنَّمَ مِنَ الجِنَّةِ وَالنَّاسِ اجمَعِينَ ***"Certainly shall I fill Hellfire with jinn and men all together."***[24]

---

[20]Muslim and Aḥmad.
[21]Muslim, Aḥmad and at-Tirmidhī.
[22]Sūrah al-A'rāf, 7:158.
[23]*Sūrah Saba'*, 34:28. "*Kāffah*" literally means "inclusively, without exception."
[24]*Sūrah as-Sajdah,* 32:13. See *Tafseer an-Nasafī* concerning this *āyah.* "*Al-qawl*" literally means "speech or saying." See also *Sūrah Hūd,* 11:119.

It is an indication of Allāh's knowledge that most of the people who first heard the divine message would reject it and die in a state of disbelief, thereby bringing punishment upon themselves. This is because He is fully aware of all aspects of His servants' natures, attitudes and potentials, and He knows with certainty what will be the response of each soul to the Prophet's warnings.

It should not be taken to mean, however, that they were "helpless victims of divine decree," as the fatalists would have us believe, for Allāh's knowledge of what will be in the future in no way implies that He compels one to a certain direction or deprives him of freedom and thus of responsibility. Exalted is He above any such injustice!

In reality, Allāh (ﷻ) has willed for mankind (and for the *jinn* as well) freedom of choice in matters of belief and in many decisions concerning various courses of action open to the individual. Man is taken to account only for that which is subject to his control, so those who die without having incurred responsibility (i.e., young children or the mentally deficient) are exempted of blame.[25] Whenever human will is impaired, responsibility diminishes. Therefore, Allāh has not ordered anything that man does not have the ability to carry out, and He has not prohibited anything that he is helpless to avoid. And since man himself is unaware of his own future and of his destination in the Hereafter, it cannot be said that divine knowledge has any effect upon the decisions he makes during his lifetime. When the Prophet ﷺ was asked whether there was any use in performing deeds since one's place in Heaven or Hell has already been decreed, he answered, "Work. For everyone is eased toward that for which he was created." Then he recited:

فَأَمَّا مَن أَعطَى وَاتَّقَى وَصَدَّقَ بِالحُسنَى فَسَنُيَسِّرُهُ لِليُسرَى
وَأَمَّا مَن بَخِلَ وَاستَغنَى وَكَذَّبَ بِالحُسنَى فَسَنُيَسِّرُهُ لِلعُسرَى

"Those who give, are conscious [of Allāh], and believe in the good reward – We shall ease them towards ease. But as for those who withhold [what they have], consider themselves self-sufficient, and deny the good reward – We shall ease them towards difficulty."[26]

Ibn Katheer pointed out that when one intends righteousness, Allāh rewards him by helping him to realize it. And when he intends evil, Allāh leaves him to his own devices.

Certain words of the Prophet ﷺ, although clearly perceived by his contemporaries, have been grossly misunderstood by later generations. They are part of an authentic *ḥadīth* related by Ibn Mas'ūd about creation within the womb: how the angel blows a

---

[25]The Prophet (ﷺ) said, "The pen has been lifted [i.e., does not register] for three: the sleeping one until he awakens, the boy until he reaches puberty, and the insane until he becomes sane." (al-Bukhārī and Muslim.) And he (ﷺ) also said, "My community has been excused for [unintended] mistakes, forgetting, and that which has been forced upon it." (Ibn Mājah and aṭ-Ṭabarānī –*ṣaḥeeḥ*.)
[26]Al-Bukhārī. The Qur'ānic reference is *Sūrah al-Layl,* 92:5-10.

soul into the fetus and is then ordered to write down four decrees concerning that person: his provision and sustenance on earth, his life span, his deeds, and whether he will ultimately he happy or unhappy (in the Hereafter). The Prophet ﷺ said, "By Allāh, other than whom there is no deity, indeed, one of you may do the deeds of the people of Paradise until he is only an arm's length away and then is overtaken by the decree, so he does the deeds of the people of the Fire and enters it. And one of you may do the deeds of the people of the Fire until he is only an arm's length away and then is overtaken by the decree, so he does the deeds of the people of Paradise and enters it."[27]

There are several points to be clarified concerning this *ḥadīth*:

1. It refers to a possibility. One might or could do as mentioned therein, but in the usual pattern of human behavior it is recognized that men do not suddenly change at the end of life – although it does happen occasionally.[28]

2. Allāh does not judge a person solely according to His own divine knowledge; otherwise, it could be claimed that there is no evidence to convict the guilty. A student would not readily accept the judgement of his teacher that he had failed a course in which he had not been permitted to take the required examinations. Evidence can be brought justly against (or in favor of) a particular soul only by its own witness and by that of others concerning actual occurrences.

3. The fact that a person who has lived a life of wrongdoing or disbelief can repent and change himself even in his last days, thereby gaining forgiveness and entrance into Paradise, points to the great generosity of Allāh in His acceptance of such a servant, and it shows that one should never despair of His mercy.

4. The case given of the opposite possibility (i.e., of one entering Hellfire after having lived most of his life in righteousness) is a warning to every believer to be on guard against such an occurrence. Just as one is capable of changing from evil to good and is rewarded for that, he is also responsible for keeping himself on the right path by not depending upon past deeds as sufficient for him and consequently relaxing his discipline. And further, by intending and continuing to work hard for the acceptance of Allāh – seeking His assistance in this goal up until the very last breaths of his life – he will die in a state which is pleasing to his Creator. We ask Allāh to make the best of our deeds the final ones.

Predestination (*qadar*) is an article of faith. All things are predestined by Allāh, who says: وَمَا تَشَاؤُونَ إِلا أَن يَشَاءَ الله ***"And you do not will except that Allāh wills."***[29] This means that Allāh wills that one must make a choice in particular matters. He knows beforehand what the servant will choose, and He wills whatever choice is made by that servant, whether right or wrong. The choice itself is made freely and without compulsion from Allāh. Thus human responsibility is established.

---

[27]Al-Bukhārī and Muslim.
[28]See an-Nawawī's explanation of the ḥadīth in *Ṣaḥeeḥ Muslim.*
[29]Sūrah al-Insān, 76:30.

There are those who claim that if Allāh wills a thing, then He must approve of it. But they are mistaken – for what He wills and what He likes are not necessarily the same. By way of example:

فَإِنَّ اللهَ لايُحِبُّ الكَافِرِينَ	*"Allāh does not like the disbelievers."*[30]
إِنَّ اللهَ لايُحِبُّ الـمُعْتَدِينَ	*"Indeed Allāh does not like aggressors."*[31]
وَاللهُ لايُحِبُّ الفَسَادَ	*"And Allāh does not like corruption."*[32]
وَاللهُ لايُحِبُّ الظَّالِمِينَ	*"And Allāh does not like the unjust."*[33]
إِنَّهُ لايُحِبُّ الـمُسْرِفِينَ	*"Indeed He does not like the extravagant."*[34]
إِنَّ اللهَ لايُحِبُّ الخَائِنِينَ	*"Indeed Allāh does not like traitors."*[35]
إِنَّهُ لايُحِبُّ الـمُسْتَكْبِرِينَ	*"Indeed He does not like the arrogant."*[36]

Allāh (ﷻ) has willed the existence of all of these; yet, as the *āyahs* show, He does not like any of them. He has ordered belief in and obedience to Himself, yet He has also willed the occurrence of disbelief and disobedience, which anger Him. Concerning human choice, Allāh has accordingly made known His own pleasure or displeasure. He has issued warnings and sent guidance for all who would benefit.

As for those happenings beyond a servant's control, the believer can take comfort in the fact that they, too, are predestined and willed by the just and merciful Creator. Trusting that Allāh knows best as to where true benefit lies, the servant can expect great reward for patience in hardship and difficulty:

مَا أَصَابَ مِن مُصِيبَةٍ فِي الأَرضِ وَلا فِي أَنفُسِكُم إِلا فِي كِتَابٍ مِن قَبلِ أَن نَبرَأَهَا إِنَّ ذَلِكَ عَلَى اللهِ يَسِيرٌ لِكَيلا تَأسَوا عَلَى مَا فَاتَكُم وَلا تَفرَحوا بِما آتاكُم...

"No misfortune strikes upon the earth or within yourselves except that it is in a register before We bring it into being. Indeed, that is easy for Allāh. In order that you not despair over what has eluded you and not exult [in pride] over what He has given you..."[37]

---

[30]Sūrah Āli ‘Imrān, 3:32.
[31]Sūrah al-Baqarah, 2:190.
[32]Sūrah al-Baqarah, 2:205.
[33]Sūrah Āli ‘Imrān, 3:57.
[34]Sūrah al-A‘rāf, 7:31.
[35]Sūrah al-Anfāl, 8:58.
[36]Sūrah an-Naḥl, 16:23.
[37]Sūrah al-Ḥadeed, 57:22-23.

Āyah 8

إِنَّا جَعَلْنَا فِي أَعْنَاقِهِمْ أَغْلالاً فَهِيَ إِلَى الأَذْقَانِ فَهُم مُقْمَحُونَ

Indeed, We have put shackles around their necks, which are up to their chins, so their heads are kept aloft.

Allāh (ﷻ) continues with a description of those who have deserved His decree against them. Their heads, held high in pride and disdain, have been locked into that position by shackles of stubbornness, which prevents them from submitting to the truth.

"*Aghlāl*" refers to a device used to restrain prisoners. It consists of an iron collar to which the hands are secured under the chin. Obviously, when confined in this position, one is unable to lower his head, even in humility to his Lord. Unable as well to see except in one direction, he cannot discover much of the truth around him, and with his hands chained to his neck, he cannot reach out to benefit anyone at all. Such is the prisoner of his own arrogance. Those whose heads are held up in this position are called "*muqmaḥūn.*" The same word is used for a camel which refuses to drink, stubbornly thrusting its head into the air.

The psychological state pictured so aptly in this and the following verses is an attitude of conceit, hard-heartedness and considering oneself superior. This type of personality will not accept guidance and, therefore, cannot be guided.

Āyah 9

وَجَعَلْنَا مِن بَيْنِ أَيْدِيهِمْ سَدًّا وَمِنْ خَلْفِهِمْ سَدًّا فَأَغْشَيْنَاهُمْ فَهُمْ لاَيُبْصِرُونَ

And We have put before them a barrier and behind them a barrier and covered them so they do not see.

The overall picture of total helplessness is now complete. Those who reject faith are confined by the barriers of their own prejudices and misconceptions, unable to benefit from lessons of the past or from the experience of the present. Blinded against truth and reality, they will never change their course. How dreadful is their condition!

'Ikrimah related that his father, Abū Jahl,[38] had threatened, "When I see Muḥammad, I am going to do this and that." Then Allāh revealed: ***"Indeed, we have put shackles around their necks"*** up through the words ***"...so they do not see."*** They pointed out to him, "There is Muḥammad," but he could only say, "Where is he? Where is he? I do not see him!"

---

[38]One of the Prophet's uncles, who was among the foremost of Islam's enemies.

In his *seerah* Ibn Hishām narrated that the leaders of Quraysh were assembled at night outside the house of the Prophet ﷺ, awaiting the moment to carry out his assassination. But Allāh had warned him ﷺ of their plan. While they sat in wait, the Messenger of Allāh came out. Taking a handful of earth and sprinkling it over the heads of the would-be assassins, he recited this *āyah*: ***"And We have put before them a barrier"*** to the end. Allāh turned their vision away so that they did not see him, and there remained no man among them whose head was not covered with earth. Then the Prophet ﷺ passed by them and went on to the house of Abū Bakr, from which they escaped to the cave of Thawr.

Āyah 10

وَسَوَاءٌ عَلَيهِم أَأَنذَرتَهُم أَم لَم تُنذِرهُم لايُؤمِنُونَ

And it is all the same to them whether you warn them or do not warn them – they will not believe.

These people are such that no warning can move their hearts. Here is a consolation for the Prophet ﷺ, who was often saddened by his own people's rejection of Allāh's message, and subsequently for those whose *da'wah* efforts do not always bring the desired result. The denial of clear guidance by any servant is but a penalty for previous sins and attitudes that have reached a point of no return – where no hope for righteousness remains.

This cause and effect situation in which the servant uses his free will in a rebellious manner, thereby closing the door to his own salvation, is again illustrated in other *āyahs*:

فِي قُلُوبِهِم مَرَضٌ فَزَادَهُمُ اللهُ مَرَضًا

"There is illness in their hearts, so Allāh has increased them in illness."[39]

فَأَعقَبَهُم نِفَاقًا فِي قُلُوبِهِم إِلَى يَومِ يَلقَونَهُ بِمَا أَخلَفُوا اللهَ مَا وَعَدُوهُ وَبِمَا كَانُوا يَكذِبُونَ

"So He penalized them with hypocrisy in their hearts until the Day that they shall meet Him because they failed Allāh in what they promised Him and because they [habitually] used to lie."[40]

فَلَمَّا زَاغُوا أَزَاغَ اللهُ قُلُوبَهُم

"And when they turned away, Allāh turned their hearts away."[41]

---

[39]*Sūrah al-Baqarah,* 2:10. The "*illness*" mentioned here is explained as doubt, hypocrisy, arrogance and disbelief.
[40]Sūrah at-Tawbah, 9:77.
[41]Sūrah aṣ-Ṣaff, 61:5.

۞ ۞ ۞ Āyah 11 ۞ ۞ ۞

إِنَّمَا تُنذِرُ مَنِ اتَّبَعَ الذِّكْرَ وَخَشِيَ الرَّحْمَنَ بِالْغَيْبِ فَبَشِّرْهُ بِمَغْفِرَةٍ وَأَجْرٍ كَرِيمٍ

You can only warn one who follows the Remembrance and fears ar-Raḥmān unseen.
So give him good tidings of forgiveness and of generous reward.

"The Remembrance" here refers to the Qur'ān. It is so named by Allāh (ﷻ) to convey to us that its message is not new or unfamiliar. It merely reminds man of that truth already known in the depths of his own soul and witnessed at the beginning of his creation:

وَإِذْ أَخَذَ رَبُّكَ مِن بَنِي آدَمَ مِن ظُهُورِهِمْ ذُرِّيَّتَهُمْ وَأَشْهَدَهُمْ عَلَى أَنفُسِهِمْ أَلَسْتُ
بِرَبِّكُمْ قَالُوا بَلَى شَهِدْنَا أَن تَقُولُوا يَوْمَ الْقِيَامَةِ إِنَّا كُنَّا عَنْ هَذَا غَافِلِينَ

"And when your Lord took from the children of Ādam their descendants from their
loins and made them witness about themselves, [saying], 'Am I not your Lord?' They
said, 'Yes, we have witnessed' – so you cannot say on the Day of Judgement, 'Indeed
we were unaware of this...' "[42]

Every messenger was appointed by Allāh to remind men who had somehow forgotten this truth and turned away from their Lord. And each brought the same message:

قَالَ يَا قَوْمِ اعْبُدُوا اللهَ مَا لَكُم مِنْ إِلَهٍ غَيْرُهُ

"O my people, worship Allāh. You have no other god but Him."[43]

Prophethood ended with Muḥammad ﷺ, but the final Reminder to man remains until the Day of Judgement. It is complete and unaltered as promised by Allāh so that there will be no excuse for deviation and so that there will always be men who will follow the true religion:

إِنَّا نَحْنُ نَزَّلْنَا الذِّكْرَ وَإِنَّا لَهُ لَحَافِظُونَ

"Verily We have sent down the Remembrance, and verily We are its guardian."[44]

But the warning will be of no benefit to those who refuse it. In this *āyah* of *Yā Seen* the Prophet ﷺ is told by Allāh that only a certain kind of person is receptive to the warning. First, one who follows the Qur'ān, i.e., believes in it, learns it and practices it. The Prophet's companions (may Allāh be pleased with them) used to eagerly await each and every revelation, and once it was heard and understood, they would hasten to apply it to every aspect of their lives. And second, one who fears ar-Raḥmān (Allāh, the Most Merciful)[45] although he does not see Him. The Prophet ﷺ described *iḥsān* (proficiency in

---

[42]Sūrah al-A'rāf, 7:172.
[43]See *āyahs* 7:59, 7:65, 7:73, 7:85, 11:50, 11:61, 11:84 and 23:23.
[44]Sūrah al-Ḥijr, 15:9.
[45]Allāh says: قُلِ ادْعُوا اللهَ أَوِ ادْعُوا الرَّحْمَنَ أَيًّا مَا تَدْعُوا فَلَهُ الْأَسْمَاءُ الْحُسْنَى **"Call upon Allāh or call upon ar-Raḥmān. Whichever [name] you call, His are the best names."** (*Sūrah al-Isrā'*, 17:110.)

religion) as "worshipping Allāh as though you see Him, for even though you do not see Him, indeed He sees you."[46] Allāh confirms in another *āyah*:

إِنَّ الَّذِينَ يَخشَونَ رَبَّهُم بِالغَيبِ لَهُم مَغفِرَةٌ وَأَجرٌ كَبِيرٌ

"Those who fear their Lord in the unseen will have forgiveness and great reward."[47]

To such people is the Qur'ān directed – the believers ***"who, when Allāh is mentioned, their hearts are fearful; and when His verses are recited to them, their faith is increased; and upon their Lord [alone] they depend."***[48] These are the ones deserving good tidings and reassurance that all of their efforts and sacrifices in obedience to Allāh will be fully appreciated and generously rewarded by Him.

Āyah 12

إِنَّا نَحنُ نُحيِ المَوتَى وَنَكتُبُ مَا قَدَّمُوا وَآثَارَهُم وَكُلَّ شَيءٍ أَحصَينَاهُ فِي إِمَامٍ مُبِينٍ

It is We who bring the dead to life and record what they have put forth and left behind, and all things We have enumerated in a clear register.

Ibn Katheer has asserted that although the obvious meaning in this *āyah* is that Allāh will resurrect the dead on the Day of Judgement, it also contains a suggestion that He gives life to such hearts as He wills among the non-believers in the form of guidance and enlightenment after they were once "dead," i.e., in a state of unawareness and error. He has supported this view by citing *āyahs* 16 and 17 of *Sūrah al-Ḥadeed,* in which are mentioned those whose hearts had become hardened, followed by the words: ***"Know that Allāh gives life to the earth after its death. We have made evident to you the signs that perhaps you may understand."***[49] Indeed, it is well known that such outstanding men as 'Umar bin al-Khaṭṭāb and Khālid bin al-Waleed were initially enemies of Islām whose hearts were later awakened by Allāh.

The word "*mawtā*" (plural of *mayyit*), previously discussed in relation to a specific *ḥadīth,*[50] unquestionably refers in this *āyah* to "the dead," i.e., the lifeless. In other Qur'ānic verses similar in meaning to *āyahs* 10 and 11 of this *sūrah,* Allāh tells His prophet ﷺ: إِنَّكَ لاتُسمِعُ المَوتَى ***"You cannot make the dead hear,"***[51] meaning the dead of heart.

46Muslim.
47Sūrah al-Mulk, 67:12.
48Sūrah al-Anfāl, 8:2.
49*Sūrah al-Ḥadeed,* 57:17. اعلَمُوا أَنَّ اللهَ يُحيِي الأَرضَ بَعدَ مَوتِهَا قَد بَيَّنَّا لَكُمُ الآيَاتِ لَعَلَّكُم تَعقِلُونَ
50See p.2.
51Sūrah an-Naml, 27:80 and Sūrah ar-Rūm 30:52.

It is a certainty that Allāh (ﷻ) will bring the dead to life once again for the Judgement. Those who are skeptical of this fact will have their reply, but not here. It will be postponed until the final *āyahs* of the *s ūrah* after ample evidence has been provided. As for the basis of the Judgement, it is clearly stated in no uncertain terms. It will include all that one has put forth, i.e., the deeds that he has sent ahead of him to the Hereafter, either knowingly or unknowingly. And it will also include all that he did upon the earth.

The word "*āthār*" (plural of *athar*) means "traces," "effects" or "what is left behind." Thus one might say or do something (either good or evil), the effects of which will remain in the physical world or in the hearts of others for some time, perhaps even long after the person's demise. These after-effects will be a part of every servant's account.

The Prophet ﷺ explained another aspect of *āthār* when he said, "Whoever establishes a good practice [*sunnah*] in Islām[52] will have its reward and the reward of all of those who act according to it after him without lessening their rewards at all. And whoever establishes a bad practice in Islām will carry its sin and the sin of all of those who act according to it after him without lessening their sin at all."[53] And he ﷺ also stated, "When a son of Ādam [i.e., man] dies, his deeds are ended except for three: [his] knowledge from which there is benefit, a righteous child who supplicates for him, or a charity which continues on after him."[54]

Additionally, another more specific meaning also given by commentators is "footprints" or "the traces of one's footsteps," citing as an example the Prophet's advice against moving homes closer to the *masjid* since the additional steps from a distance are recorded and the person rewarded for them.

Finally, in this *āyah* Allāh (ﷻ) informs us that He keeps track of all things in a clear register (*imām*) – the Book of Deeds. And the record will be complete and accurate:

لايُغَادِرُ صَغِيرَةً وَلا كَبِيرَةً إلا أحصَاهَا

"It does not leave anything small or great except that it has enumerated it."[55]

Our familiarity in recent years with manmade devices that can record, store and later impart information to the eye and ear about many human activities and conditions must certainly facilitate understanding of this concept, although it has always been an essential part of Islamic belief. Man's ability to bring back memories of past events, complete with accompanying emotions, or the playback in a dream of something long forgotten is

[52]Note here the specification "in Islam," meaning within the guidelines laid down by Allāh and His Prophet (ﷺ). It can never include innovations in religion (*bid'ah*), which the Prophet condemned by and therefore must be classified as blameworthy practices.
[53]Muslim.
[54]Muslim.
[55]Sūrah al-Kahf, 18:49.

adequate evidence that what is past is not over and dead but continues to exist, is stored, and can be recalled whenever the Creator should will:

هَذَا كِتَابُنَا يَنطِقُ عَلَيكُم بِالحَقِّ إِنَّا كُنَّا نَستَنسِخُ مَا كُنتُم تَعمَلُونَ

"This, Our Book [of Deeds], speaks about you in truth. Verily, We were recording what you used to do." [56]

---

[56] Sūrah al-Jāthiyah, 45:29.

Section Two – Āyahs 13-32

وَاضرِب لَهُم مَثَلا أَصحَابَ القَريَةِ إِذ جَاءَهَا الـمُرسَلُونَ (١٣) إِذ أَرسَلنَا إِلَيهِمُ اثـنَينِ فَكَذَّبُوهُمَا فَعَزَّزنَا
بِثَالِثٍ فَقَالُوا إِنَّا إِلَيكُم مُرسَلُونَ (١٤) قَالُوا مَا أَنتُم إِلا بَشَرٌ مِثلُنَا وَمَا أَنزَلَ الرَّحمنُ مِن شَيءٍ إِن أَنتُم إِلا
تَكذِبُونَ (١٥) قَالُوا رَبُّنَا يَعلَمُ إِنَّا إِلَيكُم لَمُرسَلُونَ (١٦) وَمَا عَلَينَا إِلا البَلاغُ الـمُبِينُ (١٧) قَالُوا إِنَّا
تَطَيَّرنَا بِكُم لَئِن لَم تَنتَهُوا لَنَرجُمَنَّكُم وَلَيَمَسَّنَّكُم مِنَّا عَذَابٌ أَلِيمٌ (١٨) قَالُوا طَائِرُكُم مَعَكُم أَئِن ذُكِّرتُم بَل
أَنتُم قَومٌ مُسرِفُونَ (١٩) وَجَاءَ مِن أَقصَا الـمَدِينَةِ رَجُلٌ يَسعَى قَالَ يَا قَومِ اتَّبِعُوا الـمُرسَلِينَ (٢٠) اتَّبِعُوا
مَن لايَسئَلُكُم أَجرًا وَهُم مُهتَدُونَ (٢١) وَمَا لِيَ لا أَعبُدُ الَّذِي فَطَرَنِي وَإِلَيهِ تُرجَعُونَ (٢٢) أَأَتَّخِذُ مِن
دُونِهِ آلِهَةً إِن يُرِدنِ الرَّحمنُ بِضُرٍّ لاتُغنِ عَنِّي شَفَاعَتُهُم شَيئًا وَلايُنقِذُونِ (٢٣) إِنِّي إِذًا لَفِي ضَلالٍ مُبِينٍ
(٢٤) إِنِّي آمَنتُ بِرَبِّكُم فَاسمَعُونِ (٢٥) قِيلَ ادخُلِ الجَنَّةَ قَالَ يَا لَيتَ قَومِي يَعلَمُونَ (٢٦) بِمَا غَفَرَلِي
رَبِّي وَجَعَلَنِي مَنَ الـمُكرَمِينَ (٢٧) وَمَا أَنزَلنَا عَلَى قَومِهِ مِن بَعدِهِ مِن جُندٍ مِنَ السَّمَاءِ وَمَا كُنَّا مُنزِلِينَ
(٢٨) إِن كَانَت إِلا صَيحَةً وَاحِدَةً فَإِذَا هُم خَامِدُونَ (٢٩) يَاحَسرَةً عَلَى العِبَادِ مَا يَأتِيهِم مِن رَسُولٍ إِلا
كَانُوا بِهِ يَستَهزِئُونَ (٣٠) أَلَم يَرَوا كَم أَهلَكنَا قَبلَهُم مِنَ القُرُونِ أَنَّهُم إِلَيهِم لايَرجِعُونَ (٣١) وَإِن كُلٌّ لَمَّا
جَمِيعٌ لَدَينَا مُحضَرُونَ (٣٢)

(13) And put before them an example – the people of the city when the messengers came to it – (14) When We sent them two, but they denied them; so We strengthened them with a third, and they said, "Indeed we are messengers to you." (15) They said, "You are none but human beings like ourselves, and ar-Raḥmān has revealed nothing. You are only lying." (16) They said, "Our Lord knows that we are messengers to you. (17) And we are not responsible except for clear notification." (18) They said, "We consider you a bad omen. If you do not desist, we will stone you and you will be touched by a painful punishment from us." (19) They said, "Your omen is with yourselves. Is it because you were reminded? No, you are but a transgressing people." (20) And there came from the farthest end of the city a man, running. He said, "O my people, follow the messengers. (21) Follow those who do not ask of you any payment and are [rightly] guided. (22) And why should I not worship the One who created me and to whom you shall return? (23) Should I take [for myself] deities other than Him when if ar-Raḥmān means for me some adversity their intercession will not avail me at all, nor can they save me? (24) I would then certainly be in manifest error. (25) Verily, I have believed in your Lord, so listen to me." (26) It was said, "Enter Paradise." He said, "I wish my people could know... (27) ...of how my Lord has forgiven me and made me among the honored." (28) And We did not send down upon his people after him any soldiers from Heaven, nor would We have done so. (29) It was not but a single blast and they were [immediately] extinguished. (30) Alas for the servants. No messenger comes to them except that they ridicule him. (31) Do they not see how many generations We have destroyed before them – that they will not return to them? (32) But all of them will yet be brought into Our presence.

The Effect of Stories in the Qur'ān

Being the words of Allāh (*subḥānahu wa ta'ālā*), Qur'ānic narrations contain pure, historic truths free from the fantasy and imaginings found in the works of human authors. Allāh confirms: وَالَّذِي أَوحَينَا إِلَيكَ مِنَ الكِتَابِ هُوَ الحَقُّ... **"And that which We have inspired to you of the Scripture is the truth."**[57] The Qur'ān makes use of the story's natural attraction to impart certain lessons and implant them in the mind of the reader or listener.

There are three types of stories related in the Qur'ān:

1. Those about prophets
2. Those about ancient peoples or events
3. Those about events which occurred during the time of Prophet Muḥammad ﷺ

Sūrah Yā Seen contains a unique account belonging to the second category, in which the result of rejection and rebellion is exposed as well as that of faith and *jihād.*

Āyah 13

وَاضرِب لَهُم مَثَلا أَصحَابَ القَريَةِ إِذ جَاءَهَا المُرسَلُونَ

And put before them an example – the people of the city when the messengers came to it

"And put before them an example..." Allāh (ﷻ) orders His Prophet ﷺ to give this illustration from the past which has been revealed to him. The Qur'ānic style brings the scene before its audience almost as though they are eyewitnesses.

"...The people of the city when the messengers came to it..." Although some early commentators relying upon Christian sources have held that this city was Antioch and that the messengers were sent by Prophet 'Eesā (peace be upon him), there is no support for this view in the Qur'ān or in any authentic *ḥadīth.* On the contrary, in refuting it Ibn Katheer has cited well-known historical facts as counter-evidence.[58] Since the objective behind Qur'ānic stories is to remind, warn and advise, the naming of specific places would normally not serve any useful purpose. Allāh (ﷻ) does not distract from the narration of this story with unnecessary details but goes directly on to the point of the lesson.

---

[57]Sūrah Fāṭir, 35:31.

[58]In any case, Christian and Jewish sources cannot be considered valid unless confirmed in the Qur'ān or in *ḥadīths.*

Āyah 14

إِذ أَرسَلنَا إِلَيهِمُ اثنَينِ فَكَذَّبُوهُمَا فَعَزَّزنَا بِثَالِثٍ فَقَالُوا إِنَّا إِلَيكُم مُرسَلُونَ

When We sent them two, but they denied them; so We strengthened them with a third, and they said, "Indeed we are messengers to you."

Here is a settlement to which Allāh had sent two messengers. Before the Final Scripture was revealed to Prophet Muḥammad ﷺ, messengers were sent to peoples who had forgotten their Creator (worshipping and obeying others besides Him) and had strayed into evil and corruption. One can only speculate as to why a single messenger was not sufficient for this particular community. Nevertheless, we are informed that since two were denied, Allāh saw fit to reinforce them with a third. The messengers immediately and publicly announce themselves, for their message (and that of all prophets and of the propagators after them) is a clear and direct one without mystery or deception: ***"Indeed we are messengers to you."***

Āyah 15

قَالُوا مَا أَنتُم إِلا بَشَرٌ مِثلُنَا وَمَا أَنزَلَ الرَّحمنُ مِن شَىءٍ إِن أَنتُم إِلا تَكذِبُونَ

They said, "You are none but human beings like ourselves, and ar-Raḥmān has revealed nothing. You are only lying."

These three statements put forward by the obstinate people reflect and summarize the position of those who reject the divine message in every generation. If they had been open to guidance, the disbelievers of Quraysh would surely have seen their own attitudes reflected in this dialogue. When following the story through to its conclusion, they would have found adequate warning about the danger of similar behavior towards any messenger sent by Allāh – in particular the one who was then among them ﷺ.

The three arguments alleged by the rejecters are as follows:

1) ***"You are none but human beings like ourselves."***

The disbelievers suppose that any messenger coming from Allāh should be an angel or a supernatural being. Allāh states:

وَمَا مَنَعَ النَّاسَ أَن يُؤمِنُوا إِذ جَاءَ هُمُ الهُدَى إِلا أَن قَالُوا أَبَعَثَ الله بَشَرًا رَسُولاً

"And what prevented the people from believing when guidance came to them except that they said, 'Has Allāh sent a human messenger?!' "[59]

[59]Sūrah al-Isrā', 17:94.

Prophet Nūḥ faced the same objection,[60] as did Hūd,[61] Ṣāliḥ[62] and Muḥammad ﷺ.[63] "Because they are human beings like ourselves, we cannot accept them as messengers from Allāh," declared their opponents.

In their pretense of intelligence and sophistication, the objectors forget a simple fact – that education by demonstration is an essential aspect of the revelation. Any creature other than a man could not reasonably be accepted as a pattern of conduct and behavior. One could easily justify failure to practice a way of life taught by an angel or other type of being. The vast difference between its physical and psychological nature and that of man would be cited as a prohibiting factor. In His wisdom, Allāh (ﷻ) willed that certain men (i.e., His messengers) should not only expound but also demonstrate the practical application of divine teachings. The fact that those human beings were given the special capacity for reception of messages from the Creator of the universe far beyond the limits of creation is surely no less a miracle than what the skeptics demand, but their minds and hearts are closed to the obvious truth.

The Qur'ān states simply that every messenger ever sent to earth by Allāh was a human being.[64] It argues:

قُل لَوكَانَ فِي الأَرضِ مَلائِكَةٌ يَمشُونَ مُطمَئِنِّينَ لَنَزَّلنَا عَلَيهِم مِنَ السَّمَاءِ مَلَكًا رَسُولاً

"Say, 'If there were angels walking securely upon the earth, We would have sent down to them from Heaven an angel as a messenger.' "[65] Thus, a human messenger is most suitable as an example to the earth's human inhabitants.

2) ***"Ar-Raḥmān has revealed nothing."***

Even if they admit the existence of a Creator, as most of the ancients did, their denial that He would continue to care for His creatures and communicate His will to them leads the complacent to reject revelation and prophethood. Sensing that a message from Allāh Almighty could not be ignored, they chose to completely avoid confrontation with responsibility by claiming that He never sent down any such message in the first place. In Sūrah al-Mulk the inhabitants of Hellfire confess to this, saying:

قَالُوا بَلَى قَد جَاءَنَا نَذِيرٌ فَكَذَّبنَا وَقُلنَا مَا نَزَّلَ اللهُ مِن شَيءٍ إِن أَنتُم إِلا فِي ضَلالٍ كَبِيرٍ

"Yes, a warner had come to us, but we denied and said, 'Allāh has revealed nothing. You are but in a great delusion.' "[66]

---

[60]See Sūrah al-Mu'minūn, 23:24.
[61]See Sūrah al-Mu'minūn, 23:33-34.
[62]See Sūrah al-Qamar, 54:24.
[63]See Sūrah al-Furqān, 25:7.
[64]See Sūrah al-Anbiyā', 21:7-8 and Sūrah al-Furqān, 25:20.
[65]Sūrah al-Isrā', 17:95.
[66]Sūrah al-Mulk, 67:9.

3) ***"You are only lying."***

By accusing the messengers of falsehood, the arrogant ones seek to prevent the development of trust in them among the population. They have begun to feel the threat that the truth would bring to their evil establishment. Those intruders must be discredited in order to preserve the status-quo, in short, the community's worldly interests and institutions based upon tyranny and oppression.

Āyah 16

قَالُوا رَبُّنَا يَعلَمُ إِنَّا إِلَيكُم لَمُرسَلُونَ

They said, "Our Lord knows that we are messengers to you."

Sufficient is the knowledge of Allāh. If no one should believe them, the messengers will do their duty in any case, seeking His reward. Man is charged with effort, but the end result is in the hands of Allāh (*subḥānahu wa ta'ālā*).

Āyah 17

وَمَا عَلَينَا إِلا البَلاغُ المُبِينُ

"And we are not responsible except for clear notification."

Confidently, the messengers state that they are aware of the limits of their responsibility. They have conveyed the information entrusted to them by Allāh and fulfilled their duty, and after that the people are free to decide for themselves. But a wrong decision made by them in spite of clear warnings cannot be blamed upon the messengers.

Āyah 18

قَالُوا إِنَّا تَطَيَّرنَا بِكُم لَئِن لَم تَنتَهُوا لَنَرجُمَنَّكُم وَلَيَمَسَّنَّكُم مِنَّا عَذَابٌ أَلِيمٌ

They said, "We consider you a bad omen. If you do not desist, we will stone you and you will be touched by a painful punishment from us..."

The evil ones are becoming increasingly anxious. They call upon the ignorant and superstitious nature of the population, hoping to attach a stigma to the three messengers by suggesting that they will be a cause of ill fortune[67] and, therefore, should be eliminated. The call to righteousness and to the worship of Allāh must be aborted if their own social system is to survive. The oppressors will not tolerate reformers among them. If they cannot discredit them or discourage them with harsh words, then stronger measures will be taken.

Thus, as it does in every age, tyranny exposes its own failure. It cannot withstand the expression of truth or even of the least bit of criticism. Opposition must be silenced. Power and authority in the land must be retained at all costs. The people must not think of change; they must not hear of it. They must not know that it is possible. They must believe that in their present situation all is well... or at least that nothing is better. They must be protected from alien influence, from insurgents who question corrupt authority, undermine security and sow discontentment.

Tyranny cannot allow the outspoken bearers of truth to go unchecked. It is helpless against reason and cannot hope to persuade. It can only strike out violently in frustration and anger. Any threat of such action should be taken very seriously indeed. The messengers are warned: Either cease your *da'wah* efforts or expect the worst!

Āyah 19

قَالُوا طَائِرُكُم مَعَكُم أَئِن ذُكِّرتُم بَل أَنتُم قَومٌ مُسرِفُونَ

They said, "Your omen is with yourselves. Is it because you were reminded? No, you are but a transgressing people."

The response of the messengers is again a simple truth. Superstition is a pastime of the ignorant, who are unable to relate events to their proper causes, who refuse to admit failures, and who claim that any ill which befalls them is due to an evil spirit or some unaccountable foreign influence. Often they seek to blame others for agitating that mysterious force against them. But, in reality, one's fate is in his own hands in as much as the decision is his whether to follow the guidance imparted by Allāh and reap its benefit or to reject it and bear the consequences. The people are told: Any evil that should befall you after this information has reached you is merely the result of your own misdeeds and bad intentions.

[67]The word "*taṭayyarnā*" is derived from "*ṭāra*" (طَارَ), meaning "flew." Among the ancient superstitions was the one that a bird be released if an important decision was to be made. If it flew to the left, it was seen as a bad omen.

And pointing directly to the example before them, the messengers put the question: ***"Is it because you were reminded?"*** Do you reward those who care for your own best interests, reminding you of all that is good and warning you against that which is harmful, with defiance, slander and threat? For our exertion on your behalf you would stone us and torture us? ***"No, you are but a transgressing people,"*** exceeding all limits of justice and decency.

Āyah 20

وَجَاءَ مِن أَقصَا المَدِينَةِ رَجُلٌ يَسعَى قَالَ يَا قَومِ اتَّبِعُوا المُرسَلِينَ

And there came from the farthest end of the city a man, running. He said, "O my people, follow the messengers."

It is possible, as some commentators have suggested, that at this point the defiant community was about to kill the three messengers. In contrast to their violent reaction against the truth is this example of a true believer who exerts himself in its defense.

A lone man driven by sense of duty propels himself towards the gathering in the center of town. He has heard the message and understood it. Its appeal to reason has opened his eyes. Its evidence is such as to leave no doubt. Certain that the warnings are true and concerned for his people's welfare, he cannot remain silent. Not wasting a moment with introductions or pleasantries, he comes straight to the point: ***"O my people, follow the messengers."***

Āyah 21

اتَّبِعُوا مَن لا يَسئَلُكُم أَجرًا وَهُم مُهتَدُونَ

"Follow those who do not ask of you any payment and are [rightly] guided."

The believer points out that the messengers are not seeking any worldly gain for all of their trouble. This is surely proof of sincerity and truthfulness, for who would undertake such a thankless task otherwise? Who would oppose familiar traditions to which the people are attached and will defend blindly? Who would expose himself to ridicule and insult, bearing the anger and assault of the disbelievers with no compensation in this world... unless he expected a greater reward from another source? All prophets sent by Allāh to mankind have clarified their position to the people, saying:

وَمَا أَسْئَلُكُم عَلَيهِ مِن أَجرٍ إِن أَجرِىَ إِلا عَلَى رَبِّ العَالَمِينَ

"And I do not ask of you any payment for it. My payment is only from the Lord of the Worlds."[68]

The fact that they are rightly guided is plain from the nature of their message, for they invite only to the worship of one God, who is the Creator of mankind and of all things. Their creed is clear and simple, free of mystery, secrecy or superstition. Compatible with *fiṭrah*[69] and with human nature, it satisfies both the heart and the intellect. And there is adequate evidence to support it, whether in the visible universe or within the human person himself:

سَنُرِيهِم آيَاتِنَا فِي الآفَاقِ وَفِي أَنفُسِهِم حَتَّى يَتَبَيَّنَ لَهُم أَنَّهُ الحَقُّ

"We shall show them Our signs in the horizons and within themselves until it becomes evident to them that it is the truth."[70]

Āyah 22

وَمَا لِىَ لا أَعبُدُ الَّذِي فَطَرَنِي وَإِلَيهِ تُرجَعُونَ

"And why should I not worship the One who created me and to whom you shall return?"

The believer appeals to his people's reason and common sense. Using himself as an example to illustrate his point, he responds to their implied question: What! Should we abandon what our fathers worshipped for the worship of Allāh alone? He answers with questions of his own: Does it stand to reason that while Allāh has created me, sustains me and controls my destiny I should worship other than Him? Would I not then be ungrateful and undeserving of His favor? And since you as well as I will ultimately return to our Creator, would it not be foolish on our part to avoid establishing a good relationship with Him?

Prophet Muḥammad ﷺ was directed by Allāh to use a similar argument and say:

فَلا أَعبُدُ الَّذِينَ تَعبُدُونَ مِن دُونِ اللهِ وَلَكِنْ أَعبُدُ اللهَ الَّذِي يَتَوَفَّاكُم

"I do not worship those whom you worship other than Allāh, but I worship Allāh, who takes your souls."[71]

---

[68]*Sūrah ash-Shu'arā'*, 26:109. See also *āyahs* 127, 145, 164 and 180.

[69]The natural inclination of man to worship his Creator before his → corruption by external influences. The Prophet (ﷺ) said, "Every newborn child is born with *fiṭrah*. Then his parents make him a Jew, a Christian or a Majūsī." (al-Bukhārī and Muslim.)

[70]Sūrah Fuṣṣilat, 41:53.

[71]Sūrah Yūnus, 10:104.

❧ ❧ ❧ Āyah 23 ❧ ❧

أَأَتَّخِذُ مِن دُونِهِ آلِهَةً إِن يُرِدْنِ الرَّحمنُ بِضُرٍّ لاتُغْنِ عَنِّي شَفَاعَتُهُم شَيْئًا وَلاَيُنقِذُونِ

"Should I take [for myself] deities other than Him when if ar-Raḥmān means for me some adversity their intercession will not avail me at all, nor can they save me?"

Going on to expose the error in a position which opposes the natural, instinctive and reasonable object of worship, the believer states that no power can prevent what Allāh, ar-Raḥmān, has willed. "So," he asks, "why waste one's time and effort on false and impotent gods?"

Taking a deity for oneself involves the question of authority, since the basis of worship is obedience. Who should have the right to govern man if not the One who created him and knows him better than he knows himself? But man, in his ignorance and injustice, readily gives his loyalty to other "authorities" – to humans like himself, customs, traditions, political ideologies, fashionable trends, material possessions and physical passions – raising them by his devotion to the status of gods, enslaving himself to serve them, and ultimately degrading his own humanity. Yet none of these can save one from misfortune, if willed by Allāh (ﷻ):

وَإِن يَمْسَسْكَ اللهُ بِضُرٍّ فَلا كَاشِفَ لَهُ إِلا هُوَ

"If Allāh touches you with adversity, no one can remove it except Him."[72]

Allāh is completely superior to and unlike anything He has created. He alone is the cause of all that takes place in creation – the original source of all things and all occurrences. Totally dependent upon Allāh for his continued existence on earth and then for His mercy in the Hereafter, man is in no logical position to invite His anger.

To the claim of those who say they merely worship others as intermediaries, the believer adds that the intercession of false gods is useless. Allāh confirms:

أَمِ اتَّخَذُوا مِن دُونِ اللهِ شُفَعَاءَ. قُل أَوَلَوْكَانُوا لاَيَمْلِكُونَ شَيْئًا وَلاَيَعْقِلُونَ. قُل لِّلهِ الشَّفَاعَةُ جَمِيعًا لَهُ مُلْكُ السَّمَاوَاتِ والأَرضِ ثُمَّ إِلَيهِ تُرجَعُونَ

"Or do they take as intercessors other than Allāh? Say, 'Even though they cannot control anything nor can they reason?!' Say, 'To Allāh belongs [the right to allow] intercession entirely. To Him belongs the dominion of the heavens and the earth. Then [finally] to Him you will be returned.'"[73]

And He says:

مَن ذَا الَّذِي يَشْفَعُ عِندَهُ إِلا بِإِذْنِهِ

"Who is it that can intercede with Him except by His permission?"[74]

---

[72]Sūrah al-An'ām, 6:17 and Sūrah Yūnus, 10:107.
[73]Sūrah az-Zumar, 39:43-44.
[74]Sūrah al-Baqarah, 2:255.

Āyah 24

إِنِّي إِذًا لَفِي ضَلَالٍ مُبِينٍ

"I would then certainly be in manifest error."

After putting forth his case based upon reason, the believing man concludes his argument: How could I accept deities other than ar-Raḥmān, Allāh, Most Merciful, when He is the only one worthy of my worship and obedience? It is obvious that I as well as anyone who should prefer an inferior alternative would be making a grave misjudgement. Then he confirms that he has taken the only course open to an intelligent person, urging his people to do the same...

Āyah 25

إِنِّي آمَنتُ بِرَبِّكُم فَاسمَعُونِ

"Verily, I have believed in your Lord, so listen to me."

Thus speaks the believer, standing courageously before the crowd, knowing that whatever the outcome, Allāh is with him, hearing and seeing, witnessing his efforts and his testimony. Surely his reward cannot be far away...

Āyah 26

قِيلَ ادخُلِ الجَنَّةَ قَالَ يَالَيتَ قَومِي يَعلَمُونَ

It was said, "Enter Paradise." He said, "I wish my people could know..."

Martyrdom is not obtained easily. Such men as this believer are chosen by Allāh for the honor after having proven their worthiness.

The abrupt transfer in scene from that earthly confrontation to the Hereafter conveys the meaning that the believer's death was immediate and at the hands of those he had tried to guide. Ibn Katheer has related, "When he said that [i.e., ***"Verily, I have believed in your Lord, so listen to me."***], they leaped upon him with one leap and killed him, and there was no one to defend him." Ibn Mas'ūd mentioned that they trampled him under their feet. And Qutādah said, "They began throwing stones at him while he kept saying, 'O Allāh, guide my people, for they know not,' until they slew him – may Allāh have mercy upon him."

However the tragedy occurred, the ugly and violent death suggested here along with previous background information serves to portray the depths of depravity to which man is capable of sinking when he disassociates himself from divine guidance and consciousness of Allāh. How often have similar scenes taken place in the past and present, in public and private – the hysterical frenzy of human beasts who cannot bear truth and justice. Angry, contorted faces thirsty for blood, consumed with hatred for those whose only crime is that they accept the authority of Allāh above all else. When Fir'aun disclosed his intention to kill Prophet Mūsā (peace be upon him), another believing man stood up in his defense with a word of truth: أَتَقْتُلُونَ رَجُلًا أَن يَقُولَ رَبِّيَ اللهُ وَقَدْ جَاءَكُم بِالْبَيِّنَاتِ مِن رَّبِّكُمْ ***"Do you kill a man [only] because he says, 'My lord is Allāh' and has brought you evidences from your Lord?"***[75] And al-Bukhārī related that when one of the idol-worshippers attacked the Prophet ﷺ near the *Ka'bah,* trying to strangle him with the Prophet's own clothing, Abū Bakr rushed in to prevent him, weeping and shouting out the aforementioned *āyah* from beginning to end.

Submission to the will of Allāh, the Exalted, by any sector of society has always been a problem for the ignorant majority and is viewed by them as a danger. Clearly, truth and falsehood are incompatible and cannot tolerate each other. About those who drove men, women, and children into trenches of fire for refusing to renounce their religion, Allāh (ﷻ) said: وَمَا نَقَمُوا مِنْهُمْ إِلَّا أَن يُؤْمِنُوا بِاللهِ الْعَزِيزِ الْحَمِيدِ

"And they took not revenge against them except [for] that they believed in Allāh, the Almighty, the Praiseworthy."[76]

Any individual or community whose lord is Allāh will never accept a human substitute or an inferior ideal. Here the threat to traditional, materialistic culture becomes evident. The enemies of Allāh are helpless against Him. They can only vent their frustrations against His sincere servants, but in doing so they merely hasten and increase His reward to them.

Thus, the believing man's death sustained for the cause of Allāh has made Paradise due to him. He is told without delay, "Enter Paradise." His murder at the hands of the hostile oppressors is the vehicle which carries him from the world of trial, hardship and fear to that of peace, security and honor.

Despite his painful experience, the martyred believer bears no ill feeling toward his murderers. He is not their enemy but simply the enemy of their transgressions. If only they could be made aware of the countless blessings and rewards awaiting the faithful so that they could change their ways. ***"I wish my people could know...,"*** he says...

---

[75]Sūrah Ghāfir, 40:28.
[76]Sūrah al-Burūj, 85:8.

~ ~ Āyah 27 ~ ~

بِمَا غَفَرَ لِي رَبِّي وَجَعَلَنِي مِنَ الْمُكْرَمِينَ

"...of how my Lord has forgiven me and made me among the honored."

The Qur'ān has given a glimpse into the Hereafter to reassure us that in spite of his apparent defeat at the hands of the aggressors, the believer's struggle to uphold truth was not in vain. For there he is, enjoying rewards far beyond what he had earned through the mercy of Allāh – and sufficient to be mentioned at this time is the forgiveness and honor which has been bestowed upon him.

In Ibn Isḥāq's *seerah* it is related that Musaylimah the Liar[77] interrogated Ḥabeeb bin Zayd concerning the Prophet ﷺ and then said to him, "Do you testify that he is the messenger of Allāh?" "Yes," replied Ḥabeeb. He said, "Do you testify that I am the messenger of Allāh?" "I do not hear," was the reply. So Musaylimah (may the curse of Allāh be upon him) said, "So, you hear that [question] but do not hear this one?!" "Yes," he replied. Thereupon he had his limbs cut off, joint by joint, repeating the question each time. But he gained nothing by it... until finally his victim expired. Upon hearing that the martyr's name was Ḥabeeb, Ka'b al-Aḥbār said, "And by Allāh, the name of the man in *Yā Seen* was Ḥabeeb." But Allāh knows best.[78]

~ ~ Āyah 28 ~ ~

وَمَا أَنزَلْنَا عَلَىٰ قَوْمِهِ مِن بَعْدِهِ مِن جُندٍ مِّنَ السَّمَاءِ وَمَا كُنَّا مُنزِلِينَ

And We did not send down upon his people after him any soldiers from Heaven, nor would We have done so.

The believer had met the result of his efforts – the eternal reward of Paradise. As for the defiant ones, their fate was sealed by their own evil actions, just as the messengers had foretold. For Allāh (ﷻ) did not even consider them worth sending angels to punish them, as had been done with other evil communities. Said Ibn Mas'ūd, "It was much simpler than that." Those who had denied Allāh's messengers and killed His faithful servant met with a vengeance swifter than their own...

[77]Musaylimah al-Kadh-dhāb (the Liar) was an impostor who claimed prophethood during the lifetime of Muḥammad (ﷺ).
[78]Quoted from Ibn Katheer.

Āyah 29

إِن كَانَت إِلا صَيحَةً وَاحِدَةً فَإِذَا هُم خَامِدُونَ

It was not but a single blast and they were [immediately] extinguished.

Commentators have explained that Allāh disdained to send His army of angels to deal with such a despicable population. Rather, He brought about their destruction by a mere shout from Jibreel, causing them to collapse and die at once, just as a raging fire is extinguished, leaving no trace except dead ashes.

Āyah 30

يَا حَسرَةً عَلَى العِبَادِ مَا يَأتِيهِم مِن رَسُولٍ إِلا كَانُوا بِهِ يَستَهزِئُونَ

Alas for the servants. No messenger comes to them except that they ridicule him.

Alas, how regretful![79] One can only regret the condition of such servants of Allāh, who, instead of receiving His messengers with joy and gratitude, reject and belittle them. These servants will be filled with regret in the Hereafter when they experience the punishment that they deserve and which could have been avoided. They will further regret the eternal loss of Paradise, which could have been theirs if they had not refused it. Allāh (ﷻ) opened the doors of His mercy by sending them His messengers, but they, in turn, only received them with rudeness and injury. Now there is no further chance for repentance – only bitterness, self-reproach and pain.

Āyah 31

أَلَم يَرَوا كَم أَهلَكنَا قَبلَهُم مِنَ القُرُونِ أَنَّهُم إِلَيهِم لا يَرجِعُونَ

Do they not see how many generations We have destroyed before them – that they will not return to them?

Will they not benefit from previous examples? The question is addressed to any and all who think that they can escape the justice of their Lord – the evil community described in this *sūrah,* the Quraysh in their opposition to Prophet Muḥammad ﷺ, or the tyrants and oppressors of every age, who persecute and pour vengeance upon those who seek to establish Allāh's law upon the earth.

---

[79] "*Yā ḥasrah*" literally means "O regret!"

Have any of them ever returned to the world to enjoy the fruits of their endeavors? Or have they been taken away forever, seized by the Angel of Death and dragged unwillingly out of this life to face the anger of their Creator, who says:

نُمَتِّعُهُم قَلِيلاً ثُمَّ نَضطَرُّهُم إِلَى عَذَابٍ غَلِيظٍ

"We grant them enjoyment for a little; then We shall force them to a massive punishment."[80]

The Prophet ﷺ said, "Allāh, exalted is He, extends the time of the oppressor, but when He seizes him, He will not let him escape." Then he recited:

وَكَذَٰلِكَ أَخْذُ رَبِّكَ إِذَا أَخَذَ الْقُرَىٰ وَهِيَ ظَالِمَةٌ إِنَّ أَخْذَهُ أَلِيمٌ شَدِيدٌ

"And thus is the seizure of your Lord when He seizes the cities while they are transgressing. Verily His seizure is painful and severe."[81]

Āyah 32

وَإِن كُلٌّ لَمَّا جَمِيعٌ لَدَيْنَا مُحضَرُونَ

But all of them will yet be brought into Our presence.

Every people and every nation from the past, present and future will be brought forward for their account on the Day of Judgement, stripped of all their authority and earthly possessions. "That day Allāh will fold up the heavens in His right hand and fold up the earth in His left hand, saying, 'I am the Sovereign. Where are the tyrants? Where are the arrogant?!' "[82]

With this notice the narration is concluded, leaving every heart to reflect upon its lesson.

---

[80]Sūrah Luqmān, 31:24.
[81]Muslim. The Qur'ānic reference is *Sūrah Hūd,* 11:102.
[82]Portion of a *ḥadīth* related by Muslim.

Section Three – Āyahs 33-44

وَآيَةٌ لَهُمُ الأَرْضُ الْمَيْتَةُ أَحْيَيْنَاهَا وَأَخْرَجْنَا مِنْهَا حَبًّا فَمِنْهُ يَأْكُلُونَ (٣٣) وَجَعَلْنَا فِيهَا جَنَّاتٍ مِن نَخِيلٍ
وَأَعْنَابٍ وَفَجَّرْنَا فِيهَا مِنَ الْعُيُونِ (٣٤) لِيَأْكُلُوا مِن ثَمَرِهِ وَمَا عَمِلَتْهُ أَيْدِيهِمْ أَفَلا يَشْكُرُونَ (٣٥) سُبْحَانَ الَّذِي
خَلَقَ الأَزْوَاجَ كُلَّهَا مِمَّا تُنبِتُ الأَرْضُ وَمِنْ أَنفُسِهِمْ وَمِمَّا لا يَعْلَمُونَ (٣٦) وَآيَةٌ لَهُمُ اللَّيْلُ نَسْلَخُ مِنْهُ النَّهَارَ فَإِذَا
هُم مُظْلِمُونَ (٣٧) وَالشَّمْسُ تَجْرِي لِمُسْتَقَرٍّ لَهَا ذَلِكَ تَقْدِيرُ الْعَزِيزِ الْعَلِيمِ (٣٨) وَالْقَمَرَ قَدَّرْنَاهُ مَنَازِلَ حَتَّى
عَادَ كَالْعُرْجُونِ الْقَدِيمِ (٣٩) لا الشَّمْسُ يَنبَغِي لَهَا أَن تُدْرِكَ الْقَمَرَ وَلا اللَّيْلُ سَابِقُ النَّهَارِ وَكُلٌّ فِي فَلَكٍ
يَسْبَحُونَ (٤٠) وَآيَةٌ لَهُمْ أَنَّا حَمَلْنَا ذُرِّيَّتَهُمْ فِي الْفُلْكِ الْمَشْحُونِ (٤١) وَخَلَقْنَا لَهُم مِّن مِثْلِهِ مَا يَرْكَبُونَ (٤٢)
وَإِن نَشَأْ نُغْرِقْهُمْ فَلا صَرِيخَ لَهُمْ وَلا هُمْ يُنقَذُونَ (٤٣) إِلا رَحْمَةً مِّنَّا وَمَتَاعًا إِلَى حِينٍ (٤٤)

(33) And a sign for them is the dead earth. We have brought it to life and brought forth from it seeds from which they then eat. (34) And We made therein gardens of date-palms and grapes and caused springs to burst forth therefrom (35) So that they may eat of its fruit. And their hands have not produced it, so will they not give thanks? (36) Praise be to Him who created all pairs – from what the earth grows and from themselves and from that which they do not know. (37) And a sign for them is the night. We strip from it the day, so they are left in darkness. (38) And the sun runs on course towards its final destination. That is the calculation of the Almighty, the All-Knowing. (39) And the moon – We have determined for it phases until it returns [appearing] like an old date stalk. (40) It is not for the sun to reach the moon, nor does the night overtake the day, but each swims in an orbit. (41) And a sign for them is that We carried their forefathers in a laden ship. (42) And We created for them from the likes of it that which they ride. (43) And if We willed, We could drown them; then no helper [responding to their cry] would there be, nor would they be saved – (44) Except as a mercy from Us and provision for a time.

"And a Sign for Them..."

Within the following *āyahs* are proofs, not only of the Creator's unlimited power and ability but of His unity as reflected in creation. These *āyahs* are truly signs of Allāh from Allāh. Although they initially draw man's attention to that which is completely familiar to him, they contain information only recently understood and appreciated after scientific research led to new and amazing discoveries. Being the final revelation to mankind, the Qur'ān has been made a continuing miracle by Allāh containing evidence to be uncovered gradually as men increase in knowledge of their universe.

The Qur'ān is not and was never meant to be a book of scientific facts, as such. It is a book of guidance, merely mentioning certain realities recognized by men both at the time of revelation and again in later centuries – realities submitted as evidence and proof which cannot be denied. Ironically, the most notable of these proofs have been exposed to the world in recent years by non-believers, who pride themselves on scientific achievement and who do not consider themselves in need of religion. With the exception of a few honest souls among them who have been guided to faith, the egotism and arrogance of many researchers has prevented them from benefiting from the signs of Allāh manifest before their very eyes.

But for those hearts and souls open to the truth, understanding comes easily, and they are seized with awe and reverence. For even that portion of the universe now known to man through observation and calculation is much more complex and mysterious than we can imagine. Undoubtedly, every new discovery in the world of matter, energy, time and space can only increase the believer in faith and humility towards Him who devised, projected and systematized such a plan and then assigned to mankind his place within it, giving him the noble role of Allāh's representative upon the earth.

Some Muslims, although harboring good intentions, have fallen into the error of seeking to "prove" the Qur'ān's authenticity with modern scientific findings. In reality, the Qur'ān is itself a final statement – the absolute divine criterion by which all other statements and theories can be judged. Conversely, those "facts" accepted by science today are neither final nor absolute.

The scientific miracle of the Qur'ān does not lie merely in its allusion to certain physical realities, but more in its advocation of the research, study, thought and contemplation that leads humanity to faith by actual conviction rather than blind acceptance. The Qur'ān urges man to consider the signs in all of creation, including his own self, thus giving him guidelines for the sound thinking which leads to correct conclusions. Allāh states:

سَنُرِيهِم آيَاتِنَا فِي الأَفَاقِ وَفِي أَنفُسِهِم حَتَّى يَتَبَيَّنَ لَهُم أَنَّهُ الحَقُّ أَوَلَم يَكفِ بِرَبِّكَ أَنَّهُ
على كُلِّ شَيءٍ شَهِيدٌ

"We shall show them Our signs in the horizons and within themselves until it becomes evident to them that it is the truth. But then, is it not sufficient that your Lord is witness over all things?"[83]

---

[83]Sūrah Fuṣṣilat, 41:53.

Āyah 33

وَآيَةٌ لَهُمُ الأَرضُ المَيتَةُ أَحيَينَاهَا وَأَخرَجنَا مِنهَا حَبًّا فَمِنهُ يَأكُلُونَ

And a sign for them is the dead earth. We have brought it to life and brought forth from it seeds from which they then eat.

The word "*āyah*" is used here to convey its general meaning of "sign" or "evidence" of a certain truth given by Allāh (ﷻ). Thus, an *āyah* (verse) from the Qur'ān is included in this general meaning as well, for every Qur'ānic *āyah* is a sign from Allāh to mankind complementing those signs manifest in the physical universe.

"And a sign for them" who have denied the messengers of Allāh, who remain unmoved by the lessons of past generations and who do not understand the point behind the fact mentioned in the previous verse – that they will leave this world never to return – ***"a sign for them is the dead earth. We have brought it to life."*** The sign presented is evidence of the Creator, who recreates and gives life to that which is seemingly dead. The prophets and messengers have imparted such information while inviting mankind to Allāh. But, in reality, all creation speaks of Allāh, providing countless examples of His unlimited power and creative ability.

Here is the earth directly before the eyes of men and under their feet. They see it in periods of drought, burned and parched,[84] with no signs of life on its surface. Then they see it come alive with green sprouts and small creatures within hours after a life-giving rainfall. Allāh describes it thus:

وَتَرَى الأَرضَ هَامِدَةً فَإذَا أَنزَلنَا عَلَيهَا المَاءَ اهتَزَّت وَرَبَت وَأَنبَتَت مِن كُلِّ زَوجٍ بَهِيجٍ

"And you see the earth lifeless. Then when We send down upon it water, it quivers and swells and grows [something]of every beautiful kind."[85]

The miracle of life reoccurring periodically before the human eye, the production of a tiny seed from which life begins anew, the variation of seeds and grains which give sustenance and nourishment to men as well as other creatures, the atmospheric properties causing suitable conditions for life and growth upon the earth, and the dependence of those conditions upon such external factors as the earth's relationship to the sun – all of these are evidence of an intricate plan devised by a supreme Creator.

---

[84]In colder climates the earth appears lifeless when frozen over with ice or snow.

[85]Sūrah al-Ḥajj, 22:5.

✿ ✿ Āyah 34 ✿ ✿

وَجَعَلْنَا فِيهَا جَنَّاتٍ مِن نَخِيلٍ وَأَعْنَابٍ وَفَجَّرْنَا فِيهَا مِنَ الْعُيُونِ

And We made therein gardens of date-palms and grapes and caused springs to burst forth therefrom –

Some of the seeds will be eaten, some will be lost due to unfavorable conditions, and some will grow to produce vegetation, fruits and new seeds, by Allāh's will. Man might take for granted his provisions from the earth, but if he observes and considers carefully, he cannot fail to appreciate plant life and water which sustains it, knowing that he is completely dependent upon the perpetuation of these blessings for him by Allāh:

وَهُوَ الَّذِي أَنزَلَ مِنَ السَّمَاءِ مَاءً فَأَخْرَجْنَا بِهِ نَبَاتَ كُلِّ شَيْءٍ فَأَخْرَجْنَا مِنْهُ خَضِرًا نُخْرِجُ مِنْهُ حَبًّا مُتَرَاكِبًا. وَمِنَ النَّخْلِ مِن طَلْعِهَا قِنْوَانٌ دَانِيَةٌ وَجَنَّاتٍ مِنْ أَعْنَابٍ وَالزَّيْتُونَ وَالرُّمَّانَ مُشْتَبِهًا وَغَيْرَ مُتَشَابِهٍ. انظُرُوا إِلَى ثَمَرِهِ إِذَا أَثْمَرَ وَيَنْعِهِ إِنَّ فِي ذَلِكُمْ لآيَاتٍ لِقَوْمٍ يُؤْمِنُونَ

"And it is He who sends down water from the sky by which We bring out the growth of all things. We produce from it greenery from which We produce seeds arranged in layers. And from the date-palm – from its emerging fruit are clusters hanging low. And [We produce] gardens of grapes and olives and pomegranates, similar yet varied. Observe its fruit when it yields and its ripening. Surely in this are signs for a people who believe."[86]

✿ ✿ Āyah 35 ✿ ✿

لِيَأْكُلُوا مِن ثَمَرِهِ وَمَا عَمِلَتْهُ أَيْدِيهِمْ أَفَلَا يَشْكُرُونَ

So that they may eat of its fruit. And their hands have not produced it, so will they not give thanks?

This intricate system was produced not only for the perpetuation of human life upon the earth but for man's enjoyment as well. Whether he eats directly from plant life or from animals dependent upon plant life, his food is a gift from the Sustainer. Men may plant and harvest by His will, but it is His hand, not theirs, that guides the tender sprout up through the darkness of the earth to the light of the sun, strengthens it and stretches it, then decorates its branches with leaves and blossoms, and ripens its fruit in preparation for consumption... *"so will they not give thanks?"* Will they not recognize the favor of Allāh, who has provided everything necessary for their survival and pleasure on earth? Or will they then turn ungratefully from Him to some other object of devotion.

Note: Some *tafseers* give an alternative meaning for this *āyah* by considering the word *"mā"* to mean "what" rather than negation. As such, the *āyah* can be read: *"So that they*

---

[86]Sūrah al-An'ām, 6:99. See also Sūrah ar-Ra'd, 13:4.

may eat from its fruit and [from] what their hands have produced [i.e., planted and harvested]." Both are grammatically correct in Arabic, although most commentators prefer the first meaning.

❧ ❧ ❧ Āyah 36 ❧ ❧ ❧

سُبْحَانَ الَّذِي خَلَقَ الأَزْوَاجَ كُلَّهَا مِمَّا تُنبِتُ الأَرْضُ وَمِنْ أَنفُسِهِم وَمِمَّا لاَيَعْلَمُونَ

Praise be to Him who created all pairs – from what the earth grows and from themselves and from that which they do not know.

The phrase *"subḥān Allāh"* (praise be to Allāh) is most often used in the Qur'ān to refute those claims which imply that Allāh is somehow in need of an associate or intermediary. It means such praise which negates imperfection and confirms that Allāh is completely free from any fault or inability ascribed to Him by the ignorant. The word of praise is used here to emphasize an important fact – the regular consistency in creation, which points to the oneness of the Creator. For in spite of the variations in types and sizes, in appearances and functions, all of creation has the same basis and form – that of duality – while the Creator alone is one.

So praise is due to Allāh alone, who created all things in pairs. These have been categorized in the *āyah* under three headings: Firstly, He has created pairs *"from what the earth grows,"* i.e., plant and animal life. Although the Arabs at the time of the Qur'ān's revelation had observed that date-palms appear to have a form of sexuality and had put this knowledge to practical use in their orchards, they could not have guessed that other plant forms contain male and female parts as well or that new life in every form is dependent upon the coming together of two opposite components.

Secondly, Allāh has created mankind in pairs *"from themselves,"* as mentioned in the *āyah*: وَمِنْ آيَاتِهِ أَنْ خَلَقَ لَكُم مِنْ أَنفُسِكُم أَزْوَاجًا لِتَسْكُنُوا إِلَيْهَا

"And among His signs is that He created for you from yourselves mates that you may find peace with them..."[87]

And thirdly, He has created pairs *"from that which they do not know."* Until recently it was not known that even lifeless matter is held together by the affinity and attraction of pairs in the form of positive and negative charges. This principle of duality, which governs the existence of our universe in such intricate precision, is mentioned by Allāh in another *āyah*:

وَمِن كُلِّ شَيْءٍ خَلَقْنَا زَوْجَيْنِ لَعَلَّكُمْ تَذَكَّرُونَ

"And from all things We have created two counterparts – that perhaps you will be reminded."[88]

---

[87]Sūrah ar-Rūm, 30:21.
[88]Sūrah adh-Dhāriyāt, 51:49.

Further examples are to be found in various phenomena observed throughout creation. Such opposites as night and day are visible and recognizable to all, while others require a particular appreciation through knowledge gained by means of special instruments or complex calculations. Needless to say, in his quest for information, mankind will continue to discover pairs about which today he has no knowledge.

Āyah 37

وَآيَةٌ لَهُمُ اللَّيلُ نَسلَخُ مِنهُ النَّهَارَ فَإِذَا هُم مُظلِمُونَ

And a sign for them is the night. We strip from it the day, so they are left in darkness.

From the earth, Allāh (*subḥānahu wa ta'ālā*) turns our attention to the heavens, beginning with a phenomenon observed regularly by the earth's inhabitants – the approach of nightfall and the disappearance of daylight. The Qur'ānic expression here is unique, for it pictures the day as a covering over the night, concealing it. Allāh then strips or peels this covering away as the earth turns in its orbit. When remembering that the original state in space is that of darkness and that light from the sun is projected onto the dark earth, one comprehends the accuracy of this description. For when any given point upon the earth turns away from the sun, the light covering its surface is removed, leaving it in its "undressed" state of darkness.

Āyah 38

وَالشَّمسُ تَجرِي لِمُستَقَرٍّ لَهَا ذَلِكَ تَقدِيرُ العَزِيزِ العَلِيمِ

And the sun runs on course towards its final destination. That is the calculation of the Almighty, the All-Knowing.

Not long ago it was assumed that the sun, being the nucleus of our solar system, was stationary, merely rotating on its axis. But now it has been shown that our sun, like other stars, is traveling through space in a single direction – rushing headlong at a speed of approximately twenty kilometers per second. Allāh (ﷻ) informs us that this phenomenon, as is the case with all creation, is a temporary state which will come to an end. Indeed, the sun will progressively run its course until it reaches a point decreed by Allāh (ﷻ). Commentators have offered two explanations concerning this "point":

1) It is a point in space (i.e., a resting place). This is also described in several

ḥadīths, such as those from *ṣaḥeeḥ al-Bukhāri* in which Abū Dharr is asked by the Prophet ﷺ, *"Do you know where the sun goes when it sets?"* and is then informed by him ﷺ, *"It goes to prostrate before its Lord beneath the Throne."* A narration by Aḥmad adds: *"...where it asks permission to rise again."* Ibn Katheer has explained, "Wherever the sun might be in relation to the earth, it will always be under the Throne of Allāh (ﷻ), which covers all of creation as a canopy. It reappears [successively around the globe] after its absence at night, by permission of Allāh." As for the sun's prostration, it might be compared to that of other forms of creation which submit obediently to His law, as mentioned in the Qur'ān:

وَالنَّجْمُ وَالشَّجَرُ يَسْجُدَانِ

"And the stars and the trees prostrate themselves."[89]

وَلِلَّهِ يَسْجُدُ مَن فِي السَّمَاوَاتِ وَالأَرْضِ طَوْعًا وَكَرْهًا وَظِلالُهُم بِالْغُدُوِّ وَالآصَالِ

"And to Allāh prostrate themselves all within the heavens and the earth, voluntarily or involuntarily, and [also] their shadows in the morning and afternoon."[90]

أَلَمْ تَرَ أَنَّ اللهَ يَسْجُدُ لَهُ مَن فِي السَّمَاوَاتِ وَمَن فِي الأَرْضِ وَالشَّمْسُ وَالْقَمَرُ وَالنُّجُومُ وَالْجِبَالُ وَالشَّجَرُ وَالدَّوَابُّ وَكَثِيرٌ مِنَ النَّاسِ

"Do you not consider that to Allāh prostrates all within the heavens and the earth – the sun, the moon, the stars, the mountains, the trees, the animals and many of the people...?"[91]

2) It is a point in time (i.e., the Day of Judgement) when the universe as we know it will end, preceding the second creation, as expressed in the words of the Qur'ān: إِذَا الشَّمْسُ كُوِّرَتْ ***"When the sun is wound up..."***[92] The sun, with its huge, flaming mass which is yet a tiny speck on the outskirts of a vast, expanding universe, is hastening on towards a specific point in time and space – a final destination – drawing its satellites (including our earth) in the same direction and at the same speed. The realization of this fact can only bring one face to face with a certain reality – his total helplessness before the will of the Creator of this entity, who has informed mankind of His plan and warned him against rebellion. ***"That is the calculation of the Almighty"*** – He who cannot be opposed or prevented from what He wills – ***"the All-Knowing,"*** who is fully aware of every movement and every stillness.

[89]Sūrah ar-Raḥmān, 55:6.
[90]Sūrah ar-Ra'd, 13:15.
[91]Sūrah al-Ḥajj, 22:18.
[92]Sūrah at-Takweer, 81:1.

༺ ༺ Āyah 39 ༻ ༻

وَالْقَمَرَ قَدَّرْنَاهُ مَنَازِلَ حَتَّى عَادَ كَالْعُرْجُونِ الْقَدِيمِ

And the moon – We have determined for it phases until it returns [appearing] like an old date stalk.

Again man is reminded of an occurrence which he witnesses repeatedly throughout his lifetime – the successive stages of the moon, by which the months are recognized, just as the sun provides the standard of measure for days and nights. As Allāh mentions in other *āyahs*:

هُوَ الَّذِي جَعَلَ الشَّمسَ ضِيَاءً وَالقَمَرَ نُورًا وَقَدَّرَهُ مَنَازِلَ لِتَعلَمُوا عَدَدَ السِّنِينَ وَالحِسَابَ

"It is He who has made the sun a shining light and the moon a reflected light and determined for it phases – that you may know the number of years and account [of time]."[93]

وَجَعَلنَا اللَّيلَ وَالنَّهَارَ آيَتَينِ فَمَحَونَا آيَةَ اللَّيلِ وَجَعَلنَا آيَةَ النَّهَارِ مُبصِرَةً لِتَبتَغُوا فَضلاً مِن رَبِّكُم لِتَعلَمُوا عَدَدَ السِّنِينَ وَالحِسَابَ وَكُلَّ شَيءٍ فَصَّلنَاهُ تَفصِيلاً

"And We have made the night and day [as] two signs. Then We erased the sign of the night and made the sign of the day visible – that you may seek favors from your Lord and know the number of years and account [of time]. And everything We have set forth in complete detail."[94]

يَسئَلُونَكَ عَنِ الأَهِلَّةِ. قُل هِيَ مَوَاقِيتُ لِلنَّاسِ وَالحَجِّ

"They ask you about the new moons. Say, 'They are [to determine] times for the people and for ḥajj...' "[95]

The moon is born as a crescent, and then it grows night after night until it becomes full and bright. Then it begins to decrease until it is once more a crescent shape – but this time with a difference. For the new moon appears with a glow of freshness and youth, but the waning moon fades as in old age, reminding the observer of a dried date stalk which has withered into a thin, sickle shape. It is not by chance that the Qur'ān uses this particular description.[96]

---

[93]Sūrah Yūnus, 10:5.
[94]Sūrah al-Isrā', 17:12.
[95]Sūrah al-Baqarah, 2:189.
[96]Fī Thilāl il-Qur'ān, p. 2969.

Āyah 40

لا الشَمسُ يَنبَغِي لَهَا أَن تُدرِكَ القَمَرَ وَلا اللَّيلُ سَابِقُ النَّهَارِ وَكُلٌّ فِي فَلَكٍ يَسبَحُونَ

It is not for the sun to reach the moon, nor does the night overtake the day, but each swims in an orbit.

Up until recent times the sun and the moon seemed to the earth's inhabitants to be following a similar course – each in turn – rising in the east and setting in the west. The frequent appearance of the moon during daylight hours gives an additional allusion of nearness at times.

Yet Allāh affirmed in the Qur'ān long before the advent of modern science that the sun cannot make contact with the moon, nor can the sequence of night and day be affected, since each of these bodies is restricted to its own orbit, unable to escape or to alter the path ordained for it – neither transgressing its limit nor falling behind.

Besides the precision of their orbits, the vast distances between each of the heavenly bodies serves to offset the effect of gravity, which would otherwise pull them into a collision course. These distances are hard to imagine even today. The moon is a mere 387,000 kilometers from our earth, while the sun is 150 million kilometers away. Yet these figures are insignificant when compared to the distance between our galaxy and that nearest to us, estimated at about 167 million million kilometers or four light years.[97] Between the cluster to which our galaxy belongs and that next to it is a distance of some fifty million light years. These clusters have been observed in every direction that one can look into space – moving rapidly away from us and from each other:

وَالسَّمَاءَ بَنَينَاهَا بِأَيدٍ وَإِنَّا لَمُوسِعُونَ

"And the heavenly structure – We have constructed it with strength, and it is We who expand [it]."[98]

So for as long as the Creator wills, great distances and precision of orbits will prevent the sun from reaching the moon or the night overtaking the day. The orbits themselves are described by the word "*falak*," which was explained by Ibn 'Abbās and others as resembling the cog wheels of a weaving tool commonly used at that time, which do not rotate except conjointly in a mutual relationship.

The movement of each body in its orbit is further described in the Qur'ān as "swimming." Such are the realities revealed by the Creator of the heavens and the earth to His unlettered prophet over fourteen centuries ago:

---

[97]A light year is the distance light travels through space in one year at the speed of almost 300,000 kilometers per second or 9.484 trillion kilometers.

[98]Sūrah adh-Dhāriyāt, 51:47.

إِنَّ اللهَ يُمسِكُ السَّمَاوَاتِ وَالأَرضَ أَن تَزُولا وَلَئِن زَالَتَا إِن أَمسَكَهُمَا مِن أَحَدٍ مِن بَعدِهِ

"Surely does Allāh hold the heavens and the earth, lest they cease. And if they should cease, none can hold them after Him..."[99]

Āyah 41

وَآيَةٌ لَهُم أَنَّا حَمَلنَا ذُرِّيَّتَهُم فِي الفُلكِ المَشحُونِ

And a sign for them is that We carried their forefathers in a laden ship.

In a subtle allusion to a common law governing the floating of stars and planets in space and that of ships on water, Allāh (ﷻ) turns our attention to yet another sign – the ark which carried Prophet Nūḥ and the few believers among his people over the flood waters to safety. For it was under divine inspiration and instruction that he constructed this first ship which served as a model for later vessels.

We are reminded that not only did Allāh favor man by teaching him how to cross rivers and seas but also that He saved the faithful who had accompanied Nūḥ in the ark, making them the forefathers of all men to be born after them. The waters which had destroyed the evildoers were at once a blessing for the believers by Allāh's will. Indeed, by His will, all favors are granted and all knowledge is gained. Referring to this event in the Qur'ān, He addresses mankind:

إِنَّا لَمَّا طَغَا المَاءُ حَمَلنَاكُم فِي الجَارِيَةِ. لِنَجعَلَهَا لَكُم تَذكِرَةً وَتَعِيَهَا أُذُنٌ وَاعِيَةٌ

"Verily, when the water overflowed, We carried you in the [moving] ship – that We might make it a reminder for you and that it might be understood by understanding ears."[100] Thus, as an additional favor, all believers can benefit from the lessons of the past related to them by Allāh.

Āyah 42

وَخَلَقنَا لَهُم مِن مِثلِهِ مَا يَركَبُونَ

And We created for them from the likes of it that which they ride.

Although one interpretation states that this creation refers to camels or other beasts of burden, the more generally accepted explanation is that it means those ships which were later fashioned from the pattern of the first ark. Since the source of all human knowledge

---

[99]Sūrah Fāṭir, 35:41.

[100]Sūrah al-Ḥāqqah, 69:11-12.

and ability is Allāh, He aptly describes man's work as His creation. In the words of Prophet Ibrāheem: وَاللهُ خَلَقَكُمْ وَمَا تَعمَلُونَ ***"And Allāh created you and that which you do."***[101]

◆ ◆ Āyah 43 ◆ ◆

وَإِن نَشَأْ نُغرِقهُم فَلا صَرِيخَ لَهُم وَلا هُم يُنقَذُونَ

And if We willed, We could drown them; then no helper [responding to their cry] would there be, nor would they be saved

Here is a further reminder to those who through pride and confidence in their own achievements forget themselves and their debt to Allāh. For it is He who has given them life and sustenance and then knowledge and skill, enabling them to sail the seas in search of His bounty. Yet He could just as well withdraw His protection at any instant, exposing them to terror and sudden death.[102] Every individual is safeguarded whether on land or at sea simply because Allāh (*subḥānahu wa ta'ālā*) has willed his existence to continue for a specified period ***"to test you as to which of you is best in deed."***[103]

◆ ◆ Āyah 44 ◆ ◆

إلا رَحمَةً مِنَّا وَمَتَاعًا إِلَى حِينٍ

Except as a mercy from Us and provision for a time

Were it not for the mercy of Allāh, no one could survive the violent and all-encompassing forces of nature. If not for the mercy of Allāh, life could not continue. Yet He grants this extension to provide every soul with opportunities for accepting the truth, for repenting from sin or for increasing in righteousness until the appointed time for return unto Him.

But in spite of those mentioned and of countless other great signs, mankind remains in a state of unconsciousness, forgetting Allāh except in periods of anxiety and distress:

---

[101] Sūrah aṣ-Ṣāffāt, 37:96.
[102] See *Sūrah al-Isrā'*, 17:66-70.
[103] *Sūrah al-Mulk*, 67:2. {لِيَبلُوَكُم أَيُّكُم أَحسَنُ عَمَلاً}

فَإِذَا رَكِبُوا فِي الفُلْكِ دَعَوُا الله مُخلِصِينَ لَهُ الدِّينَ فَلَمَّا نَجَّاهُم إِلَى البَرِّ إِذَا هُم يُشرِكُونَ. لِيَكفُرُوا بِمَا آتَينَاهُم
وَلِيَتَمَتَّعُوا فَسَوفَ يَعلَمُونَ

"Then if they board a ship, they supplicate Allāh, sincere in religion [i.e., devotion] to Him. But when He delivers them to land, they associate others with Him. So let them deny what We have granted them, and let them enjoy themselves – for they are going to know."[104]

Section Four – Āyahs 45-54

وَإِذَا قِيلَ لَهُمُ اتَّقُوا مَا بَينَ أَيدِيكُم وَمَا خَلفَكُم لَعَلَّكُم تُرحَمُونَ (٤٥) وَمَا تَأْتِيهِم مِن آيَةٍ مِن آيَاتِ رَبِّهِم إِلا
كَانُوا عَنهَا مُعرِضِينَ (٤٦) وَإِذَا قِيلَ لَهُم أَنفِقُوا مِمَّا رَزَقَكُمُ الله قَالَ الَّذِينَ كَفَرُوا لِلَّذِينَ آمَنُوا أَنُطعِمُ مَن لَو
يَشَاءُ الله أَطعَمَهُ إِن أَنتُم إِلا فِي ضَلالٍ مُبِينٍ (٤٧) وَيَقُولُونَ مَتَى هَذَا الوَعدُ إِن كُنتُم صَادِقِينَ (٤٨)
مَايَنظُرُونَ إِلا صَيحَةً وَاحِدَةً تَأخُذُهُم وَهُم يَخِصِّمُونَ (٤٩) فَلا يَستَطِيعُونَ تَوصِيَةً وَلا إِلَى أَهلِهِم
يَرجِعُونَ (٥٠) وَنُفِخَ فِي الصُّورِ فَإِذَا هُم مِنَ الأَجدَاثِ إِلَى رَبِّهِم يَنسِلُونَ (٥١) قَالُوا يَا وَيلَنَا مَن بَعَثَنَا
مِن مَرقَدِنَا. هَذَا مَا وَعَدَ الرَّحمنُ وَصَدَقَ المُرسَلُونَ (٥٢) إِن كَانَت إِلا صَيحَةً وَاحِدَةً فَإِذَا هُم جَمِيعٌ
لَدَينَا مُحضَرُونَ (٥٣) فَاليَومَ لاتُظلَمُ نَفسٌ شَيئًا وَلاتُجزَونَ إِلا مَا كُنتُم تَعمَلُونَ (٥٤)

(45) But when it is said to them, "Beware of that before you and that after you so perhaps you will receive mercy..." (46) And no sign comes to them from the signs of their Lord except that they turn away therefrom. (47) And when it is said to them, "Spend from that with which Allāh has provided you," the unbelievers say to the believers, "Should we feed him whom if Allāh had willed He would have fed? You are not but in manifest error." (48) And they say, "When is this promise, if you should be truthful?" (49) They await not except one blast; it will seize them while they are disputing. (50) Then they will not be able to give any instruction, nor can they return to their people. (51) And the Horn shall be blown; then [immediately] they will hasten from their graves to their Lord. (52) They will say, "O ruined are we! Who has raised us up again from our beds?! This is what ar-Raḥmān had promised, and the messengers have told the truth." (53) It is not but one blast and they are all brought present before Us. (54) So today no soul will be wronged at all, and you will not be penalized except for what you used to do.

---

[104] Sūrah al-'Ankabūt, 29:65-66.

༄ Āyah 45 ༄

وَإِذَا قِيلَ لَهُمُ اتَّقُوا مَا بَيْنَ أَيْدِيكُم وَمَا خَلْفَكُم لَعَلَّكُم تُرحَمُونَ

But when it is said to them, "Beware of that before you and that after you so perhaps you will receive mercy..."

"That before you" is expressed in Arabic literally as "that between your hands," i.e., what you already have. Early scholars have defined "that before" one and "that after" him thus:

That before	That after
Past sins	Future sins
Lessons from history	What will be in the Hereafter
The portion of life already lived	What remains of one's life span
This world	The punishment of the Hereafter
What is apparent	What is concealed

Although the sentence in this *āyah* appears incomplete, its conclusion is understood grammatically as "...they ignore the warning," the estimation being based upon the *āyah* which follows it.

From among the Creator's many manifest signs, He has given in the previous verses a few examples which are sufficient to evoke wonder and apprehension in the heart. But persons blinded by worldly distractions and self-obsession will not even notice them, much less reflect upon their significance. In His mercy, however, Allāh has not left even such souls as these without guidance but has sent messengers to point out His signs in clear language and invite them to Him. Yet despite this great favor to mankind, there remain many who refuse their Lord's invitation to mercy, reject His message and ignore His warnings.

༄ Āyah 46 ༄

وَمَا تَأْتِيهِم مِن آيَةٍ مِن آيَاتِ رَبِّهِم إِلا كَانُوا عَنهَا مُعرِضِينَ

And no sign comes to them from the signs of their Lord except that they turn away therefrom.

In spite of the countless signs of the power, ability and unity of Allāh before their very eyes, the disbelievers will continue to take them for granted, if indeed they notice them at all. Allāh confirms in a similar *āyah*:

وَكَأَيِّن مِّن آيَةٍ فِي السَّمَاوَاتِ وَالأَرضِ يَمُرُّونَ عَلَيهَا وَهُم عَنهَا مُعرِضُونَ

"And how many signs in the heavens and the earth do they pass by, yet they are turning away from them."[105]

They will neither reflect upon their significance nor take seriously those who point it out to them. They will write off those signs as mere accidents of nature or as creations brought into being without purpose. Even their own existence is seen by them as meaningless beyond the joys and hardships of this earthly life; thus they refuse to heed any suggestion of caution, while exploiting any and every opportunity for pleasure or worldly gain.

Āyah 47

وَإِذَا قِيلَ لَهُم أَنفِقُوا مِمَّا رَزَقَكُمُ اللهُ قَالَ الَّذِينَ كَفَرُوا لِلَّذِينَ آمَنُوا أَنُطعِمُ مَن لَو يَشَاءُ اللهُ أَطعَمَهُ إِن أَنتُم إِلا فِي ضَلالٍ مُبِينٍ

And when it is said to them, "Spend from that with which Allāh has provided you," the unbelievers say to the believers, "Should we feed him whom if Allāh had willed He would have fed? You are not but in manifest error."

Here is a scene from the past and the present. This *āyah* reveals a picture of the selfish, materialistic mentality which considers the well-off as deserving of Allāh's favor while those of little means are seen as less worthy. Moreover, there is an insolent attempt to shift the responsibility and blame for the condition of the needy onto Allāh, just as the polytheists did, saying: ***"If Allāh had willed, we would not have worshipped anything other than Him – neither we nor our forefathers..."***[106] But in their pretense of wit and cleverness with the assertion that one cannot tamper with fate, the shortsighted souls again overlook the fact that Allāh has willed human responsibility and accountability for all that He has commanded.

Those who decline to share their wealth, assuming that they are within their right and that they are not responsible for the plight of others, suggest that the condition of poverty is due only to laziness and incompetence. Yet inactivity, far from being an inborn trait, has been shown to be a direct result of hunger, disease and misery. Poor nutrition affects not only brain development in fetuses and children but production capacity in adults as well. Nevertheless, in recent years the destruction of surplus food stocks in Western Europe and America while millions in third-world countries are dying of hunger has been excused with the claim that supplying the needs of those people would destroy their

---

[105]Sūrah Yūsuf, 12:105.

[106]*Sūrah an-Naḥl*, 16:35. وَ قَالَ الَّذِينَ أَشرَكُوا لَو شَاءَ اللهُ مَا عَبَدنَا مِن دُونِهِ مِن شَيءٍ نَحنُ وَلا آبَاؤُنَا

motive for becoming self-sufficient! It has been estimated that a mere portion of the surplus grain fed to livestock in western countries could save all those who are dying from hunger throughout the entire underdeveloped world. As 'Alī bin Abī Ṭālib aptly said, "No poor man goes hungry except by what a rich man withholds." But food has become an instrument in the hands of the wealthy, its political utilization deemed more important than its humanitarian one.

In materialistic societies it is readily observed that the most selfish are the most successful. The world does not presently suffer from a lack of resources – only a lack of balance in distribution. But the situation will not be remedied by those who perpetrate it – those whose only aim is profit and accumulation of wealth, those who flaunt statistics while casting aside religious ethics, saying to whoever should encourage generosity and assistance to the hungry, ***"You are not but in manifest error."***

So much for the injustice of the unbelievers. This is to be expected. But what is to be said of the Muslim community?

Islam treats the issue of economic imbalance in a unique manner with both preventative and corrective measures – not simply with advice or encouragement, but with legislation. After establishing a system that guarantees just opportunities for every individual and makes work obligatory for every able-bodied man, it leaves human activity to take its course. It then counteracts any possible ill effects by requiring expenditure on the part of those who have excess until the minimum needs of all are met. In emergency situations, *ṣadaqah*, normally a charity beyond the duty of *zakāh,* becomes obligatory as well.

But unhappily, many of those who call themselves Muslims today have taken on the attitudes condemned in the Qur'ān and attributed to unbelievers. While large Muslim populations in Africa and Asia facing drought, famine, disease and death find no relief except occasionally through western aid or that of the Christian missionaries, their prosperous brothers, whose duty it is to take part in the economic uplift of the poor, continue to seek endless acquisitions and short-lived pleasures which they consider essential to their own well-being. Some even go so far as to assert that Allāh must be punishing the stricken ones for their sins, as if they themselves were faultless!

Have they forgotten that it is Allāh who has provided them with all that they possess and has, in fact, created them and all that they possess? Are they unmindful that He is able at any time He wills to reverse their fortunes or to utterly destroy them? That all of their worldly possessions as well as they themselves will one day return to Him who created them? That they will be stripped of ownership and their wealth will then be only in terms of righteous deeds and what they had once spent from their property for the pleasure of Allāh? And that all which was withheld unlawfully and unjustly will then become an inescapable and suffocating burden around their necks on the Day of

Judgement?[107] Concerning this, the Prophet ﷺ once said, "It is not poverty that I fear for you, but I fear that the earth with its comforts will be spread out for you as it was spread for those before you, that you will covet it as they coveted it, and that it will destroy you as it destroyed them."[108]

This world is but a trial – for the rich as well as the poor. When the sinners are asked in the Hereafter about what led them into Hellfire, they will list among the causes:

وَلَم نَكُ نُطعِمُ المِسكِينَ

"And we used not to feed the poor."[109]

But there will be others of Allāh's servants who had done so, saying:

إِنَّمَا نُطعِمُكُم لِوَجهِ اللهِ لانُرِيدُ مِنكُم جَزَاءً وَلا شُكُورًا

"We feed you for [the acceptance of] Allāh. We wish not from you reward nor thanks."[110]

Those are among the companions of Paradise.

During the caliphate of 'Umar bin al-Khaṭṭāb, drought struck the Arabian peninsula while the area to the north was suffering from plague. 'Umar attacked the problem of hunger effectively, never once submitting to the claim that fate is unalterable. Mobilizing food supplies from Baṣrah and from Egypt, he personally supervised distribution, temporarily suspended the legally prescribed punishment for theft (fearing that some might steal out of need) and postponed *zakāh* collection. He himself refrained from eating more than the minimum requirement and prayed with the people for rain and alleviation of their condition. He later ordered a canal to be dug between the Nile and the Red Sea to facilitate the transfer of supplies in the future. Thus, acutely aware of his responsibility before Allāh, 'Umar fought against fate with fate, in obedience to Him with the certain knowledge that exertion to change existing, adverse conditions is a noble act of worship.

Allāh addresses His servants with these words:

هَاأَنتُم هؤُلاءِ تُدعَونَ لِتُنفِقُوا فِي سَبِيلِ اللهِ فَمِنكُم مَن يَبخَلُ وَمَن يَبخَلْ فَإِنَّمَا يَبخَلُ عَن نَفسِهِ وَاللهُ الغَنِيُّ وَأَنتُمُ الفُقَرَاءُ وَإِن تَتَوَلَّوا يَستَبدِلْ قَومًا غَيرَكُم ثُمَّ لايَكُونُوا أَمثَالَكُم

"Here you are – those invited to spend in the way of Allāh – but among you are some who withhold [from greed]. And whoever withholds only withholds [benefit] from himself, and Allāh is free of need, while it is you who are in need. If you turn away [in refusal], He will replace you with another people. Then they will not be like you."[111]

---

[107]See Sūrah Āli 'Imrān, 3:180.
[108]Al-Bukhārī and Muslim.
[109]Sūrah al-Muddaththir, 74:44.
[110]Sūrah al-Insān, 76:9.
[111]Sūrah Muḥammad, 47:38.

Āyah 48

وَيَقُولُونَ مَتَى هَذَا الوَعدُ إِن كُنتُم صَادِقِينَ

And they say, "When is this promise, if you should be truthful?"

These same words have been repeated in five other *sūrahs.*[112] They reflect doubt in the hearts of those who challenge the messengers concerning the Hour of Judgement. Their question is not a request for information but merely a denial of the fact that it will ever come. It shows outright disbelief, as Allāh confirms:

يَستَعجِلُ بِهَا الَّذِينَ لايُؤمِنُونَ بِهَا وَالَّذِينَ آمَنُوا مُشفِقُونَ مِنهَا وَيَعلَمُونَ أَنَّهَا الحَقُّ

"Those who do not believe in it call for its immediate onset, but those who believe are fearful of it and know that it is the truth."[113]

Since Allāh does not disclose the time of resurrection, the disbelievers attempt to weaken the position of those who warn of it by demanding an answer they cannot give. But He (ﷻ) supplies the appropriate answer to their insolence in the following *āyahs* – informing them not *when,* but *how* it will be.

Āyah 49

مَايَنظُرُونَ إِلا صَيحَةً وَاحِدَةً تَأخُذُهُم وَهُم يَخِصِّمُونَ

They await not except one blast; it will seize them while they are disputing.

To those who question the promise of Allāh comes the answer in a few words depicting a terrible scene – one dreadful blast[114] which ends all activity upon the earth. There will be no further opportunity for repentance or for action of any kind. At the command of Allāh, the angel, Isrāfeel, will blow into the Horn, striking every living thing with terror and then death. The blast will come suddenly without warning while the people are in their markets going about their daily affairs, arguing and disputing as usual.

---

[112] 10:48, 21:38, 27:71, 34:29 and 67:25.

[113] Sūrah ash-Shūrā, 42:18.

[114] The word "ṣayḥah" translated as "blast" in this context, carries the additional meaning of "a sharp cry or shriek."

☙ ❧ ❧ Āyah 50 ❧ ❧ ☙

فَلَا يَسْتَطِيعُونَ تَوْصِيَةً وَلَا إِلَى أَهْلِهِمْ يَرْجِعُونَ

Then they will not be able to give any instruction, nor can they return to their people.

There will be no chance for counsel and no contact with families. Life will be ended utterly and completely and with it the temporary period of freewill and ability granted to man by Allāh (*subḥānahu wa ta'ālā*). The devastating blast not only terminates life on earth but signals the dissolution of the universe as a whole so that it may be replaced by a new creation suitable for the next life. How futile now are the petty schemes of men. How helpless is all creation before the divine will.

☙ ❧ ❧ Āyah 51 ❧ ❧ ☙

وَنُفِخَ فِي الصُّورِ فَإِذَا هُم مِّنَ الأَجْدَاثِ إِلَى رَبِّهِمْ يَنسِلُونَ

And the Horn shall be blown; then [immediately] they will hasten from their graves to their Lord.

This is the blast signaling the resurrection, whereupon all creatures will be brought back to life on a newly created earth. No longer in control of their own affairs, men will awaken to find themselves being assembled, all generations together, willingly or unwillingly, for the Judgement. They will at once be expelled from under the earth's surface and hurry on towards their Lord, powerless to resist.   In the Qur'ān, Allāh describes it thus:

مَا خَلْقُكُمْ وَلَا بَعْثُكُمْ إِلَّا كَنَفْسٍ وَاحِدَةٍ

"Your creation and resurrection are not except as that of a single soul..."[115]

خُشَّعًا أَبْصَارُهُمْ يَخْرُجُونَ مِنَ الأَجْدَاثِ كَأَنَّهُمْ جَرَادٌ مُّنتَشِرٌ

"They come out of the graves as if they were locusts spreading."[116]

Ibn Katheer has explained, "On the Day of Judgement the earth will be exchanged for another earth and the heavens [as well], and the dead will emerge alive from their graves by the command of Allāh and by His call to them. For He said:

ثُمَّ إِذَا دَعَاكُمْ دَعْوَةً مِّنَ الأَرْضِ إِذَا أَنتُمْ تَخْرُجُونَ

"Then when He calls you with a single call from the earth, immediately do you come forth."[117]

---

[115]Sūrah Luqmān, 31:28.
[116]Sūrah al-Qamar, 54:7.
[117]Sūrah ar-Rūm, 30:25.

Āyah 52

قَالُوا يَاوَيلَنَا مَن بَعَثَنَا مِن مَرقَدِنَا. هَذَا مَا وَعَدَ الرَّحمنُ وَصَدَقَ الـمُرسَلُونَ

They will say, "O ruined are we! Who has raised us up again from our beds?! This is what ar-Raḥmān had promised, and the messengers have told the truth."

Those who had insisted during their earthly lives that death is final and scoffed at the concept of afterlife are in a state of shock and dismay upon finding themselves reawakened in a second creation. First wondering in amazement how this came about, they cry out, "Who has raised us up from the graves in which we have lain since death?" Ibn Katheer has commented that this statement does not mean they had been resting peacefully all that time but only that the punishment of the grave which precedes the punishment of the Hellfire will be as a dream in comparison to the awesome reality of the new life.

Realizing that everything they had once denied and failed to prepare for is now coming true, the evildoers are seized with dread and apprehension: ***"This is what ar-Raḥmān had promised, and the messengers have told the truth."***

Commentators have allowed two interpretations concerning this last exclamation:

1) The angels or the believers answer the bewildered questioners by informing them that what is presently taking place is none but the fulfillment of Allāh's promise.

2) The questioners themselves now remember the divine message that they had rejected and can only bear witness that they had indeed been warned.

What can await them at this point except the justice they had once thought they would escape...

Āyah 53

إِن كَانَت إِلا صَيحَةً وَاحِدَةً فَإِذَا هُم جَمِيعٌ لَدَينَا مُحضَرُونَ

It is not but one blast and they are all brought present before Us.

Allāh confirms that there will be no delay, for as soon as life is restored to the dead, they will be brought forth before their Lord for judgement. All of this will take place during a single blast of the Horn or at one command from Allāh:

فَإِنَّمَا هِيَ زَجرَةٌ وَاحِدَةٌ فَإِذَا هُم بِالسَاهِرَةِ

"It is only a single shout and they will be [alert] upon the earth's surface."[118]

[118] Sūrah an-Nāzi'āt, 79:13-14.

Resurrection as described by Allāh in the Qur'ān is the logical conclusion to the drama of earthly life. Without it there would be no purpose in His creation of man as a reasoning, responsible being or in giving him freedom of will and action. Furthermore, there would be no need for messengers to convey His guidance and warning. But as Allāh reminds them in His reproach to those who rejected faith:

أَفَحَسِبتُم أَنَّمَا خَلَقنَاكُم عَبَثًا وَأَنَّكُم إِلَينَا لاتُرجَعُونَ

"Did you think that We had only created you uselessly and that you would not be returned to Us?"[119]

Āyah 54

فَاليَومَ لاتُظلَمُ نَفسٌ شَيئًا وَلاتُجزَونَ إِلا مَا كُنتُم تَعمَلُونَ

So today no soul will be wronged at all, and you will not be penalized except for what you used to do.

On this day (i.e., the Day of Judgement) no soul will be treated unjustly, whether righteous or rebellious. No one will be deprived of the good he earned, and no soul shall bear the burden of another. No punishment will be greater than deserved, and each will be compensated with exact justice. This is part of Allāh's mercy to all creation in general. But the believers shall have the additional mercy of forgiveness for minor sins and entrance into Paradise.

Ibn 'Abbās reported that the Prophet ﷺ said, "Allāh has recorded the good and the bad deeds. Whoever intends a good deed but does not do it – Allāh records it as a complete good deed. But if he intends it and does it, Allāh records it as ten good deeds up to seven hundred times, to many times over that. And if he intends a bad deed but does not do it, Allāh records it as a complete good deed. And if he intends it and does it, Allāh records it as one bad deed."[120]

---

[119]Sūrah al-Mu'minūn, 23:115.

[120]Al-Bukhārī and Muslim.

Section Five – Āyahs 55-68

إِنَّ أَصحَابَ الجَنَّةِ اليَومَ فِي شُغُلٍ فَاكِهُونَ (٥٥) هُم وَأَزوَاجُهُم فِي ظِلالٍ عَلَى الأَرَائِكِ مُتَّكِئُونَ (٥٦)
لَهُم فِيهَا فَاكِهَةٌ وَلَهُم مَايَدَّعُونَ (٥٧) سَلامٌ قَولاً مِن رَبٍّ رَحِيمٍ (٥٨) وَامتَازُوا اليَومَ أَيُّهَا المُجرِمُونَ
(٥٩) أَلَم أَعهَد إِلَيكُم يَابَنِي آدَمَ أَن لاتَعبُدُوا الشَّيطَانَ إِنَّهُ لَكُم عَدُوٌّ مُبِينٌ (٦٠) وَأَنِ اعبُدُونِي هَذَا صِرَاطٌ
مُستَقِيمٌ (٦١) وَلَقَدْ أَضَلَّ مِنكُم جِبِلاًّ كَثِيرًا أَفَلَم تَكُونُوا تَعقِلُونَ (٦٢) هَذِهِ جَهَنَّمُ الَّتِي كُنتُم تُوعَدُونَ (٦٣)
اصلَوهَا اليَومَ بِمَا كُنتُم تَكفُرُونَ (٦٤) اليَومَ نَختِمُ عَلَى أَفوَاهِهِم وَتُكَلِّمُنَا أَيدِيهِم وَتَشهَدُ أَرجُلُهُم بِمَا كَانُوا
يَكسِبُونَ (٦٥) وَلَونَشَاءُ لَطَمَسنَا عَلَى أَعيُنِهِم فَاستَبَقُوا الصِّرَاطَ فَأَنَّى يُبصِرُونَ (٦٦) وَلَونَشَاءُ
لَمَسَخنَاهُم عَلَى مَكَانَتِهِم فَمَا استَطَاعُوا مُضِيًّا وَلايَرجِعُونَ (٦٧) وَمَن نُعَمِّرْهُ نُنَكِّسْهُ فِي الخَلقِ أَفَلا
يَعقِلُونَ (٦٨)

(55) Indeed the companions of Paradise that Day will be amused in [joyful] occupation (56) They and their spouses, in shade, reclining on thrones. (57) For them therein is fruit and whatever they should call for (58) [And] "Peace," a pronouncement from a merciful Lord. (59) But stand apart today, you criminals. (60) Did I not enjoin upon you, O children of Ādam, that you not worship Shayṭān, for certainly he is to you a manifest enemy, (61) And [that you] worship Me? This is a straight path. (62) And he had [already] led astray from among you much of creation, so did you not have intelligence? (63) This is the Hellfire which you were promised. (64) Burn therein today for what you used to deny. (65) That day We will seal up their mouths, and their hands will speak to Us, and their feet will testify about what they used to earn. (66) Yet if We willed, We could have done away with their eyes, and they would race to reach the path, but how could they see? (67) And if We willed, We could have deformed them, [paralyzing them] in their places so they would neither be able to proceed on, nor could they return. (68) And he to whom We grant long life We reverse in creation; so will they not understand?

Āyah 55

إِنَّ أَصحَابَ الجَنَّةِ اليَومَ فِي شُغُلٍ فَاكِهُونَ

Indeed the companions of Paradise that Day will be amused in [joyful] occupation

The righteous believers, by Allāh's mercy, will not wait long for their accounts on the Day of Judgement but will pass on quickly after the announcement of their success to the reward awaiting them. As described in the Qur'ān:

فَأَمَّا مَن أُوتِيَ كِتَابَهُ بِيَمِينِهِ فَسَوفَ يُحَاسَبُ حِسَابًا يَسِيرًا وَيَنقَلِبُ إِلَى أَهلِهِ مَسرُورًا

"As for he who has been given his record in his right hand, he will be judged with an easy reckoning and return to his people in joy." [121]

They will be continually occupied with pleasures beyond the imagination of man in this worldly life – "that which no eye has seen, no ear has heard and has never occurred to a human heart."[122]

Āyah 56

هُم وَأَزوَاجُهُم فِي ظِلَالٍ عَلَى الأَرَائِكِ مُتَّكِئُونَ

They and their spouses, in shade, reclining on thrones

Enjoying a life of ease and free of discomfort, the people of Paradise share their joy with spouses most pleasing to them in the shade of gardens:

لَهُم فِيهَا أَزوَاجٌ مُطَهَّرَةٌ وَنُدخِلُهُم ظِلاً ظَلِيلاً

"For them therein are purified spouses, and We will admit them to deepening shade." [123]

مُتَّكِئِينَ فِيهَا عَلَى الأَرَائِكِ لايَرَونَ فِيهَا شَمسًا وَلا زَمهَرِيرًا

"Reclining therein on thrones, they will see therein neither [burning] sun nor [freezing] cold." [124]

---

[121] Sūrah al-Inshiqāq, 84:7-9.
[122] Al-Bukhārī, Muslim and others.
[123] Sūrah an-Nisā', 4:57.
[124] Sūrah al-Insān, 76:13.

Āyah 57

لَهُم فِيهَا فَاكِهَةٌ وَلَهُم مَايَدَّعُونَ

For them therein is fruit and whatever they should call for

Concerning the fruits of Paradise, Ibn Jareer has commented that they resemble those of our earth in appearance but are far superior in taste. And Ibn 'Abbās said, "What is in Paradise does not resemble what is [known] in this world except in name." But Allāh knows best about this. He says:

كُلَّمَا رُزِقُوا مِنهَا مَن ثَمَرَةٍ رِزقًا قَالُوا هَذَا الَّذِي رُزِقنَا مِن قَبلُ وَأُتُوا بِهِ مُتَشَابِهًا

"Whenever they are provided with a provision of fruit therefrom, they say, 'This is what we were provided with before.' And it is given to them in likeness."[125]

Yet the provisions with which the righteous are rewarded are not limited to fruits but certainly include whatever the soul desires and more:

وَلَكُم فِيهَا مَا تَشتَهِي أَنفُسُكُم وَلَكُم فِيهَا مَا تَدَّعُونَ

"And for you therein is whatever your souls long for, and for you therein is whatever you call for."[126]

فَأُولَـئِكَ يَدخُلُونَ الجَنَّةَ يُرزَقُونَ فِيهَا بِغَيرِ حِسَابٍ

"Those will enter Paradise, being given provision therein without measure."[127]

Āyah 58

سَلامٌ قَولاً مِن رَبٍّ رَحِيمٍ

[And] "Peace," a pronouncement from a merciful Lord

In addition to their pleasures, the righteous will be comforted by the word of peace from Allāh (*subḥānahu wa ta'ālā*). And Ibn 'Abbās pointed out that Allāh Himself is peace upon the people of Paradise. This *āyah* is similar in meaning to another in which Allāh promises: تَحِيَّتُهُم يَومَ يَلقَونَهُ سَلامٌ ***"Their greeting the day they meet Him will be 'Peace.'"***[128]

What could be more desired by the believing soul after its long struggle upon the earth against tyranny, greed and malice than peace – relief from harm and from pain and from animosity – refuge in the eternal peace of Allāh (*subḥānahu wa ta'ālā*).

125Sūrah al-Baqarah, 2:25.
126Sūrah Fuṣṣilat, 41:31.
127Sūrah Ghāfir, 40:40.
128Sūrah al-Aḥzāb, 33:44.

Āyah 59

But stand apart today, you criminals. وَامْتَازُوا الْيَوْمَ أَيُّهَا الْمُجْرِمُونَ

The people of Paradise have passed on to their home of eternal peace and happiness after a brief and easy reckoning. Now attention is turned to the evildoers, who are told to separate and remove themselves from the ranks of the believers, making their shameful position clear to all and depriving them of any benefit that they might have hoped for had they remained in the company of those covered by the mercy of Allāh. It is has been suggested further by some scholars that the criminals are told to separate from each other into the heretical sects and parties to which they had belonged in the world and to be identified with them. As Allāh says:

وَيَوْمَ تَقُومُ السَّاعَةُ يَوْمَئِذٍ يَتَفَرَّقُونَ

"And the day the Hour is established – on that Day they will separate."[129]
In other words, they will disperse, divide and be differentiated from one another. Moreover, they will be separated from those they had once followed, worshipped or obeyed other than Allāh:

وَيَوْمَ نَحْشُرُهُمْ جَمِيعًا ثُمَّ نَقُولُ لِلَّذِينَ أَشْرَكُوا مَكَانَكُمْ أَنْتُمْ وَشُرَكَاؤُكُمْ فَزَيَّلْنَا بَيْنَهُمْ

"One day We shall gather them all together; then We will say to those who associated [others with Allāh], 'Stay in your place, you and those you associated.' And We will disperse them."[130]

Isolated and helpless, they await the dreaded account of their misdeeds.

Āyah 60

أَلَمْ أَعْهَدْ إِلَيْكُمْ يَابَنِي آدَمَ أَنْ لَاتَعْبُدُوا الشَّيْطَانَ إِنَّهُ لَكُمْ عَدُوٌّ مُبِينٌ

"Did I not enjoin upon you, O children of Ādam, that you not worship Shayṭān, for certainly he is to you a manifest enemy"

The evildoers are brought forward to face the displeasure and anger of Allāh, Lord of the Worlds. Having rejected His warning and guidance, preferring instead those unlawful ways once made to seem pleasing by Shayṭān, they are now severely reproached for their foolishness in disobeying the Almighty Creator. Addressing them as "children of Ādam," Allāh alludes not only to the well-known treachery of Shayṭān in tempting and deceiving their first ancestor and his mate but also to His warning to them:

---

[129]Sūrah ar-Rūm, 30:14.
[130]Sūrah Yūnus, 10:28.

يَابَنِي آدَمَ لايَفتِنَنَّكُمُ الشَّيطَانُ كَمَا أَخرَجَ أَبَوَيكُم مِنَ الجَنَّةِ

"O children of Ādam, do not let Shayṭān seduce you as he removed your parents from the Garden."[131]

إِنَّ الشَّيطَانَ لَكُم عَدُوٌّ فَاتَّخِذُوهُ عَدُوًّا

"Certainly, Shayṭān is an enemy to you, so take him as an enemy."[132]

They had carelessly disregarded the open declaration of war on mankind by Shayṭān, who, disdaining righteousness and mercy, had defiantly vowed to lead to destruction any and all who would follow him in disobedience to Allāh.

All commentators have stated with certainty that worship of Shayṭān means obeying him in disobedience to ar-Raḥmān. The Qur'ān declares in the words of Prophet Yūsuf:

إِنِ الحُكمُ إِلا لِلّهِ أَمَرَ أَلاَّ تَعبُدُوا إِلا إِيَّاهُ

"Legislation is only for Allāh. He has commanded that you not worship any but Him."[133]

The true, comprehensive definition of "worship" is "submission and obedience." There should be no obedience to any created being which involves disobedience to the Creator, yet Shayṭān invites mankind to oppose divine legislation. By obedience to his agents, the worship of Shayṭān is realized, just as obedience to those authorities upholding the law of Allāh is, in fact, worship of Him. Those guilty ones who now stand humbled and humiliated in the Hereafter preferred to follow their own desires or the conceptions of other men in opposition to divine law and thus became worshippers of Shayṭān.

Had the transgressors accepted truth and returned to Allāh in repentance, He would have covered them with His mercy and protected them from their enemy. For He has reassured man that it is within his power to avoid seduction by Shayṭān:

إِنَّهُ لَيسَ لَهُ سُلطَانٌ عَلَى الَّذِينَ آمَنُوا وَعَلَى رَبِّهِم يَتَوَكَّلُونَ إِنَّمَا سُلطَانُهُ عَلَى الَّذِينَ يَتَوَلَّونَهُ وَالَّذِينَ هُم بِهِ مُشرِكُونَ

"Indeed there is no authority for him [i.e., Shayṭān] over those who believe and trust in their Lord. His authority is only over those who turn to him [in obedience] and those who, through him, worship others [than Allāh]."[134]

---

[131]Sūrah al-A'rāf, 7:27.
[132]Sūrah Fāṭir, 35:6.
[133]Sūrah Yūsuf, 12:40.
[134]Sūrah an-Naḥl, 16:99-100.

Āyah 61

وَأَنِ اعْبُدُونِي هَٰذَا صِرَاطٌ مُّسْتَقِيمٌ

"And [that you] worship Me? This is a straight path."

Among scholars' general definitions of "the straight path" is that taken from this *āyah*: the worship of Allāh. In the Qur'ān, He (ﷻ) has informed us of the purpose for which man was created: وَمَا خَلَقْتُ الْجِنَّ وَالإِنسَ إِلا لِيَعْبُدُونِ ***"And I did not create the jinn and mankind except to worship Me."***[135] In Islam, worship (*'ibādah*) is not limited to prayer, fasting, *zakāh* and *ḥajj*. It is impossible that the ultimate purpose of man's creation could be realized through acts which require only a minor portion of his time and resources. If the remainder of one's existence outside of these four "pillars" is not worship, then life surely falls short of the purpose stated by Allāh. On the other hand, it is beyond the ability of man to spend his entire existence in formal rites of worship or in continuous praise of Allāh throughout the day and night, as do the angels. Therefore, logically as well as linguistically, the concept of worship must include all of a servant's motivations and actions throughout his lifetime. Additionally, Allāh states in the Qur'ān that He created man in order to test him,[136] and this trial entails how completely he will fulfill the purpose for which he was created. He commands:

إِنَّ هَٰذِهِ أُمَّتُكُمْ أُمَّةً وَاحِدَةً وَأَنَا رَبُّكُمْ فَاعْبُدُونِ

"This, your community, is one community, and I am your Lord so worship Me,"[137] meaning, through *tawḥeed,* obedience and striving for the acceptance and pleasure of Allāh.

"This is a straight path" leading directly to Him for those who so desire. As Allāh states in another *āyah*:

وَأَنَّ هَٰذَا صِرَاطِي مُسْتَقِيمًا فَاتَّبِعُوهُ وَلاتَتَّبِعُوا السُّبُلَ فَتَفَرَّقَ بِكُمْ عَن سَبِيلِهِ

"And this is My path, which is straight, so follow it. And do not follow [other] ways so that you would be separated from My way."[138]

And He warns:

وَإِن تُطِعْ أَكْثَرَ مَن فِي الأَرْضِ يُضِلُّوكَ عَن سَبِيلِ اللهِ

"If you obey most of those upon the earth, they will lead you astray from the way of Allāh..."[139]

---

[135]Sūrah adh-Dhāriyāt, 51:56.
[136]See Sūrah al-Kahf, 18:7, Sūrah al-Mulk, 67:2 and Sūrah al-Insān, 76:2.
[137]Sūrah al-Anbiyā', 21:92.
[138]Sūrah al-An'ām, 6:153.
[139]Sūrah al-An'ām, 6:116.

~ ~ Āyah 62 ~ ~

وَلَقَدْ أَضَلَّ مِنكُم جِبِلاً كَثِيرًا أَفَلَم تَكُونُوا تَعقِلُونَ

"And he had [already] led astray from among you much of creation, so did you not have intelligence?"

Allāh (*subḥānahu wa ta'ālā*) continues His reproach of the criminals by reminding them of their failure to benefit from the experience of past generations. History abounds with examples of societies and nations that fell prey to Shayصān and thus met with destruction, defeat and dishonor in this world even before the next. Are these examples not sufficient to dissuade those of intelligence and perception from repeating the same errors? Many such stories are related in the Qur'ān for that very purpose, yet how many Muslims have actually opened their eyes and availed themselves of the lessons contained in them?

أَوَلَم يَسِيرُوا فِي الأَرضِ فَيَنْظُرُوا كَيفَ كَانَ عَاقِبَةُ الَّذِينَ مِن قَبلِهِم

"Did they not proceed throughout the earth and observe how was the end of those before them?"[140]

Allāh encourages believers of every generation to observe and contemplate:

فَسِيرُوا فِي الأَرضِ فَانْظُرُوا كَيفَ كَانَ عَاقِبَةُ الـمُكَذِّبِين

"So proceed throughout the earth and observe how was the end of those who denied."[141]

Today one can move about the earth from his own home – through a film, broadcast, book or newspaper – gaining information about every people and every event, past and present. Is not the handiwork of Shayṭān obvious to all?

~ ~ Āyah 63 ~ ~

هَذِهِ جَهَنَّمُ الَّتِي كُنتُم تُوعَدُونَ

"This is the Hellfire which you were promised."

The Hellfire is now brought before the condemned, just as Allāh states: وَعَرَضنَا جَهَنَّمَ يَومَئِذٍ لِّلكَافِرِينَ عَرضًا **"And We present the Hellfire that Day on display before the disbelievers."**[142] Ibn Katheer has pointed out that here Allāh indicates that He will show

---

[140]*Sūrah ar-Rūm,* 30:9 and *Sūrah Fāṭir,* 35:44. *Āyahs* 12:109, 22:46, 40:21, 40:82 and 47:10 contain the same meaning with a slight difference in wording.

[141]*Sūrah ‹li 'Imrān,* 3:137 and *Sūrah an-Naḥl,* 16:36. In 6:11, 27:69 and 30:42, the Prophet (ﷺ) is ordered to say: **"Proceed throughout the earth and observe..."**

[142]Sūrah al-Kahf, 18:100.

them the Hellfire to let them see what it contains of retribution and punishment before their entry into it. The horror of anticipation allows for even deeper regret and additional anguish.

It is related by Ibn Mas'ūd that the Prophet ﷺ said, "The Hellfire will be brought, being led from seventy thousand halters – at each one, seventy thousand angels pulling it."[143] And Abū Hurayrah reported that he ﷺ said, "The fire of Hell was burned for a thousand years until it became red. Then it was burned for a thousand years until it became white. Then it was burned for a thousand years until it became black. It is now extremely black."[144]

Āyah 64

اصلَوهَا اليَومَ بِمَا كُنتُم تَكفُرُونَ

"Burn therein today for what you used to deny."

The sentence is announced. The punishment is before them. They are powerless to resist the command, "Enter it and burn!" which is accompanied by a reminder that what is impending is none but recompense for what they themselves had earned, as their denial of Allāh had opened for them the door to every sin.

The position of those condemned to the Hellfire is further described in *Sūrah al-An'ām*:

وَلَو تَرَى إِذ وُقِفُوا عَلَى النَّارِ فَقَالُوا يَا لَيتَنَا نُرَدُّ وَلا نُكَذِّبَ بِآيَاتِ رَبِّنَا وَنَكُونَ مِنَ المُؤمِنِينَ بَل بَدَا لَهُم مَا كَانُوا يُخفُونَ مِن قَبلُ وَلَو رُدُّوا لَعَادُوا لِمَا نُهُوا عَنهُ وَإِنَّهُم لَكَاذِبُونَ

"If you could but see when they are made to stand before the Fire and they say, 'If only we could be returned [to life on earth] and not deny the signs of our Lord and be among the believers.' But that which they concealed has [now] appeared to them, and if they were returned, they would indeed return to that which they were forbidden. And certainly they are liars."[145]

---

[143]Muslim.
[144]At-Tirmidhī.
[145]Sūrah al-An'ām, 6:27-28.

Āyah 65

الْيَوْمَ نَخْتِمُ عَلَى أَفْوَاهِهِمْ وَتُكَلِّمُنَا أَيْدِيهِمْ وَتَشْهَدُ أَرْجُلُهُم بِمَا كَانُوا يَكْسِبُونَ

That day We will seal up their mouths, and their hands will speak to Us, and their feet will testify about what they used to earn.

Those who had rejected faith and the hypocrites, who pretended faith, will try to escape punishment by denying their crimes. They will attempt to defend themselves with lies and false oaths as was their habit during earthly life.[146] But Allāh will seal their mouths, silencing untruth, and cause their limbs to speak about all that they had done.

Concerning the silencing of the disbelievers, Anas bin Mālik reported, "We were with the Messenger of Allāh ﷺ, and he smiled so much that his molars appeared. Then he said, 'Do you know what I am laughing at?' We said, 'Allāh and His Messenger know most.' He said, 'At a servant's discussion with his Lord; he will say, "O Lord, will You not protect me from injustice?" and Allāh (ﷻ) will say, "Yes." So he will declare, "Then I shall not accept any witness against me except one from myself." At that, He (ﷻ) will say, "Sufficient as an accountant against you today is yourself, and as witnesses, the honorable recording angels." And his mouth will be sealed, and it will be said to the parts of his body, "Speak," and they will speak of his deeds. Then he will be allowed to talk [once again], and he will say [to his limbs], "Away with you! For it was on your behalf that I was disputing."' "[147]

Thus the evil ones find that their own bodies betray them on the Day of Judgement and oppose them with the truth. In *Sūrah Fuṣṣilat* it is further stated that their hearing, sight and skins will witness against the enemies of Allāh.[148]

وَقَالُوا لِجُلُودِهِمْ لِمَ شَهِدتُّمْ عَلَيْنَا قَالُوا أَنطَقَنَا اللهُ الَّذِي أَنطَقَ كُلَّ شَيْءٍ وَهُوَ خَلَقَكُمْ أَوَّلَ مَرَّةٍ وَإِلَيْهِ تُرْجَعُونَ

"And they will say to their skins, 'Why did you testify against us?' They will say [in reply], 'We were made to speak by Allāh, who has made everything speak, and it is He who created you and to Him you are returned.' "[149]

The senses and body members which were once under the servant's control and were misused during earthly life are no longer subject to him but only to the justice of Allāh. Ibn ʻAbbās said, "On the Day of Judgement there will come upon the people a time when they will not speak or make an excuse or utter a word until permission is granted them. Then they will dispute their judgement, and one who associated partners with Allāh will deny that he associated, and the people will swear to Him as they [now] swear to you. But while they are denying [their crimes], Allāh *taʻālā* will call forth witnesses from

---

[146]As described in *Sūrah al-Mujādilah,* 58:18.
[147]Muslim and an-Nasā'ī.
[148]See *Sūrah Fuṣṣilat,* 41:19-20.
[149]Sūrah Fuṣṣilat, 41:21.

themselves – their skins, their sight, their hands and their feet, and He will seal their mouths. Then He will open mouths in the body parts, and they [i.e., the body parts] will argue. They will say, *'We were made to speak by Allāh, who has made everything speak...'* And so the tongues will be conquered after their denial."

It is also reported by Abū Mūsā al-Ashʿarī that the disbelievers and hypocrites will say, "This angel has recorded that which I did not do." The angel will inquire, "Did you not do this-and-that on such-and-such day?" He will declare, "No, by Your power, O Lord, I did not do it." Thereupon, Allāh will seal his mouth.

If the scene portrayed in this *āyah* seems strange or inconceivable, it is, in reality, but one of the endless possibilities and alternatives to the creation which is familiar to us on the earth. The potentialities of the Hereafter far exceeding those of the present universe, nothing is beyond the all-powerful, all-capable Creator.

The verses in *Sūrah Fuṣṣilat* conclude:

وَمَا كُنتُمْ تَسْتَتِرُونَ أَن يَشْهَدَ عَلَيْكُمْ سَمْعُكُمْ وَلَا أَبْصَارُكُمْ وَلَا جُلُودُكُمْ وَلَكِن ظَنَنتُمْ أَنَّ اللهَ لَايَعْلَمُ كَثِيرًا مِّمَّا تَعْمَلُونَ وَذَلِكُمْ ظَنُّكُمُ الَّذِي ظَنَنتُم بِرَبِّكُمْ أَرْدَاكُمْ فَأَصْبَحْتُم مِّنَ الْخَاسِرِينَ

"And you were not protecting yourselves [with piety], lest your hearing witness against you or your sight or your skins, but you supposed that Allāh does not know much of what you do. And that was your supposition which you supposed about your Lord. It has brought you to ruin, and you have become among those who have lost completely."[150]

✍ ✍ Āyah 66 ✍ ✍

وَلَوْ نَشَاءُ لَطَمَسْنَا عَلَى أَعْيُنِهِمْ فَاسْتَبَقُوا الصِّرَاطَ فَأَنَّى يُبْصِرُونَ

Yet if We willed, We could have done away with their eyes, and they would race to reach the path, but how could they see?

Among the blessings usually taken for granted by man are two vital capabilities without which he would be reduced to helplessness – those of vision and movement. In human existence these facilities are meant to serve a higher purpose than they do in animals. Allāh (ﷻ) has provided through them the ability to perceive the truth and to act upon it during one's lifetime on earth. Refusal to employ them in the responsible manner befitting humanity leads to two grave consequences: the loss of these abilities even during earthly life, as described in *āyah* 9, and humiliation and punishment in the Hereafter, as revealed in *āyahs* 59-65. Allāh points out that He could just as easily have left man without a means to guidance or to the pursuit of righteousness. How miserable, then, would his condition have been.

---

[150]*Sūrah* Fuṣṣilat, 41:22-23.

The use of the verb *"ṭamasa"* (طَمَس) specifies not only that Allāh could have blinded them but that He could have completely wiped out any trace of their eyes. Ibn 'Abbās added, "He could have prevented them from guidance or from seeing the path of truth." But ar-Raḥmān, the All-Merciful, did not leave His servants to grope blindly; rather, He gave them every opportunity to benefit themselves in this world and the next.

Āyah 67

وَلَونَشَاءُ لَمَسَخنَاهُم عَلَى مَكَانَتِهِم فَمَا استَطَاعُوا مُضِيًّا وَلايَرجِعُونَ

And if We willed, We could have deformed them [paralyzing them] in their places so they would neither be able to proceed on, nor could they return.

Freedom of movement is a blessing which enables man to realize many objectives throughout life and to work for eternal happiness in the Hereafter. But if He had willed, Allāh (ﷻ) could have deprived him of this capability as well.

"*Masakha*" (مَسَخَ) carries the meaning of "petrification, transformation into a solid state or into an inferior kind of being or beast." Scholars have explained the *āyah,* saying that Allāh could have destroyed the criminals in their homes or in the place where they were committing sins, or He could have paralyzed their legs or turned them into stone. Yet He did not do so. Instead He gave them additional chances and occasions to repent and return to His grace.

The scenes of helplessness portrayed in this and the previous *āyah* are a reminder to all men of their ultimate dependence upon Allāh's favor. For as long as the body continues to function well, man is proud and confident. But once his abilities are impaired, he is forced to face the reality of his own limitations. Surely there will come a day when all human power and freedom must be relinquished to Him who granted it for a time.

Āyah 68

وَمَن نُعَمِّرْهُ نُنَكِّسْهُ فِي الخَلقِ أَفَلا يَعقِلُونَ

And he to whom We grant long life We reverse in creation; so will they not understand?

Allāh (*subḥānahu wa ta'ālā*) has already depicted the limitations of humankind in two ways – the complete loss of control over one's affairs after death and in the

Hereafter, and the possibility of incapacity during worldly life. A third limitation is mentioned here – the waning of physical and mental powers in old age. As much as man has sought to prevent it, inevitable decline and deterioration sets in visibly upon those far advanced in years. The Prophet ﷺ said, "Use medication, O servants of Allāh. For Allāh did not make an ailment but that He made a cure for it, except for one ailment: old age."[151]

The Qur'ān makes further references to the same fact:

وَمِنكُم مَن يُرَدُّ إِلَى أَرذَلِ العُمُرِ لِكَي لايَعلَمَ بَعدَ عِلمٍ شَيئًا

"And among you is he who is returned to the most decrepit [old] age so that he knows nothing after [he once had] knowledge."[152]

The reversal in creation is also described thus:

الله الَّذِي خَلَقَكُم مِن ضَعْفٍ ثُمَّ جَعَلَ مِن بَعدِ ضَعْفٍ قُوَّةً ثُمَّ جَعَلَ مِن بَعدِ قُوَّةٍ ضَعْفًا وَشَيبَةً

"It is Allāh who created you in weakness; then He made after weakness strength; then He made after strength weakness and white hair..."[153]

Reversal is evident in the emergence of weakness after strength. The aged person is in need of care and assistance to manage his affairs, as is a child before maturity. Mental function is often impaired, and emotions surface. Senility in many ways resembles the state of early childhood. Reversal is evident as well in the physical appearance of the extremely aged and in his resemblance to the unborn fetus. For Allāh created man originally from the elements of the earth and then brought him into the world through his mother's womb. One who completes a maximum life span shows the natural signs of reversal, for soon he will return to the earth, from which he came – to disintegrate and become of its elements once again, his soul awaiting the second creation as it once awaited the first. The Prophet ﷺ used to supplicate, "O Allāh, I seek refuge in You from laziness and from cowardice, from decrepitude and from stinginess" and "I seek refuge in You from being returned to the most decrepit old age."[154]

Ibn Katheer has commented about the state of this world – that it is a temporary home of transition and cessation, not a home of stability and eternity. "And for this reason," he says, "Allāh concludes: ***'...so will they not understand?'*** – meaning, will they not use their minds to think about the beginning of their creation and the process of transformation and aging in order to realize that they were created ultimately for another home, which they will never leave or be transported therefrom – the final home of the Hereafter."

---

151 Al-Bukhārī, Aḥmad and at-Tirmidhī.

152 Sūrah an-Naḥl, 16:70 and Sūrah al-Ḥajj, 22:5.

153 Sūrah ar-Rūm, 30:54.

154 Al-Bukhārī.

Section Six – Āyahs 69-83

وَمَا عَلَّمْنَاهُ الشِّعْرَ وَمَا يَنْبَغِي لَهُ إِن هُوَ إِلا ذِكْرٌ وَقُرآنٌ مُبِينٌ (٦٩) لِيُنْذِرَ مَن كَانَ حَيًّا وَيَحِقَّ الْقَوْلُ عَلَى الْكَافِرِينَ (٧٠) أَوَلَم يَرَوا أَنَّا خَلَقْنَا لَهُم مِمَّا عَمِلَت أَيْدِينَا أَنْعَامًا فَهُم لَهَا مَالِكُونَ (٧١) وَذَلَّلْنَاهَا لَهُم فَمِنْهَا رَكُوبُهُم وَمِنْهَا يَأْكُلُونَ (٧٢) وَلَهُم فِيهَا مَنَافِعُ وَمَشَارِبُ أَفَلا يَشْكُرُونَ (٧٣) وَاتَّخَذُوا مِن دُونِ اللهِ آلِهَةً لَعَلَّهُم يُنصَرُونَ (٧٤) لايَسْتَطِيعُونَ نَصْرَهُم وَهُم لَهُم جُنْدٌ مُحْضَرُونَ (٧٥) فَلا يَحْزُنْكَ قَوْلُهُم. إِنَّا نَعْلَمُ مَا يُسِرُّونَ وَمَا يُعْلِنُونَ (٧٦) أَوَلَم يَرَ الإِنْسَانُ أَنَّا خَلَقْنَاهُ مِن نُطْفَةٍ فَإِذَا هُوَ خَصِيمٌ مُبِينٌ (٧٧) وَضَرَبَ لَنَا مَثَلاً وَنَسِيَ خَلْقَهُ قَالَ مَن يُحْيِي الْعِظَامَ وَهِيَ رَمِيمٌ (٧٨) قُل يُحْيِيهَا الَّذِي أَنشَأَهَا أَوَّلَ مَرَّةٍ وَهُوَ بِكُلِّ خَلْقٍ عَلِيمٌ (٧٩) الَّذِي جَعَلَ لَكُم مِنَ الشَّجَرِ الأَخْضَرِ نَارًا فَإِذَا أَنتُم مِنْهُ تُوقِدُونَ (٨٠) أَوَلَيسَ الَّذِي خَلَقَ السَّمَاوَاتِ وَالأَرْضَ بِقَادِرٍ عَلَى أَن يَخْلُقَ مِثْلَهُم بَلَى وَهُوَ الْخَلاَّقُ الْعَلِيمُ (٨١) إِنَّمَا أَمْرُهُ إِذَا أَرَادَ شَيْئًا أَن يَقُولَ لَهُ كُن فَيَكُونُ (٨٢) فَسُبْحَانَ الَّذِي بِيَدِهِ مَلَكُوتُ كُلِّ شَيْءٍ وَإِلَيهِ تُرجَعُونَ (٨٣)

(69) And We did not give him knowledge of poetry, nor is it befitting of him. It is none other than a remembrance and a clear Qur'ān – (70) To warn whoever is alive and establish the Word against the disbelievers. (71) Do they not see that We have created for them from what Our hands have made, an'ām, and then they are their owners? (72) And We have subjected these to them; so some they ride and some they eat. (73) And there are in them [various] benefits and drink. So will they not give thanks? (74) Yet they have taken for themselves gods other than Allāh that perhaps they would be helped. (75) They are not able to help them, and, [moreover], they are soldiers in attendance for them. (76) So let not their speech grieve you. Indeed We know what they conceal and what they declare. (77) Does mankind not consider that We created him from a sperm-drop – then he has become a clear adversary? (78) He presents an example for Us and forgets his [own] creation. He says, "Who will give life to bones when they are decayed?" (79) Say, "He will give them life – who produced them the first time – and He is of all creation supreme in knowledge" – (80) The One who made for you from the green tree, fire, and then you ignite from it. (81) Is not He who created the heavens and the earth able to create the likes of them? Yes, [it is so]. And He is the omniscient Creator. (82) His command when He intends a thing is only that He says to it, "Be" and it is. (83) So praise be to Him in whose hand is the dominion of all things, and to Him you will be returned.

Āyah 69

وَمَا عَلَّمْنَاهُ الشِّعْرَ وَمَا يَنبَغِي لَهُ إِنْ هُوَ إِلا ذِكْرٌ وَقُرْآنٌ مُبِينٌ

And We did not give him knowledge of poetry, nor is it befitting of him. It is none other than a remembrance and a clear Qur'ān

In this final section, Allāh (*subḥānahu wa ta'ālā*) turns our attention once again to the three main themes of the *sūrah* – the prophethood of Muḥammad ﷺ, creation and its relationship to the Creator, and the resurrection. The subjects are mentioned briefly by way of review, yet they are presented anew with conclusive statements of evidence based upon reason and reality, which can leave no doubt in the open mind and honest heart.

The first topic dealt with is that with which the *sūrah* began – the prophethood of Muḥammad ﷺ and the nature of his message. This *āyah* contains a reply to those who claimed that the Prophet was a poet and that the Qur'ān was poetry. Those claims of the Qurayshī elite were part of a larger propaganda war launched by them against Islam and its Prophet ﷺ in an attempt to discredit him and conceal the true nature of the revelation that was coming to him. The Qur'ān documents the protests of the Quraysh:

وَيَقُولُونَ أَئِنَّا لَتَارِكُوا آلِهَتِنَا لِشَاعِرٍ مَجْنُونٍ

"And they say, 'Are we to abandon our gods for a mad poet?' "[155]

Far from being unaware of the difference between poetry and the words of the Qur'ān, they themselves were masters of poetry and completely familiar with it. Poetry was their art, their skill and their pride. The Qur'ān was clearly not in the rhythm or style of poetry, yet they were at a loss to explain the forceful attraction of its verses otherwise without making an admission that would be damaging to their position. In hopes of confusing and distracting the common people, they described it as magic or poetry – the skill of human beings or *jinn* – but nothing more.

Allāh directly refutes these allegations in this particular *āyah.* He denies giving the knowledge of poetry to the Prophet, meaning that since He did not provide such knowledge, there was no way at all it could have been obtained by him ﷺ. It was reported by those who knew him best, Abū Bakr, 'Umar and 'Ā'ishah (may Allāh be pleased with them), that the Messenger of Allāh never memorized poetry, and on occasion when he attempted to quote a verse for some reason, he usually made a mistake in it.[156]

In this *āyah* there is denial not only that the Prophet was a poet but that there was even the possibility that he could be. Allāh (ﷻ) states that it would not be proper or

---

[155] Sūrah aṣ-Ṣāffāt, 37:36.

[156] Ibn Katheer has added that the few rhyming phrases quoted from the Prophet (ﷺ) on the occasions of al-Khandaq and Ḥunayn were uttered spontaneously without his intending poetry. Furthermore, they are not confirmed as being authentic.

suitable for His messenger to be one who recited poetry. For if that were the case, some might be able to argue again that the Qur'ān was a product of his talent for verse. Another reason given by commentators is the great dissimilarity in the natures of human poetry and divine revelation and their obvious incompatibility. For even in its most civilized forms, poetry can be no more than human ideals and longings. Like any human expression, it has the capacity to serve various purposes, both noble and ignoble. As an art form, its goal is to appeal to human emotion. Yet often, as the Arabs would say, "The sweetest of it is that which is most untruthful." In particular, the Arabic poetry of that period was known for its descriptions of women, idle pastimes and immoral pleasures or for its mockery of others and attacks on their honor with the aim of arousing animosity. Whatever its purpose or potential, poetry has its own method, quite in contrast to that of prophethood.

After negating any connection between His revelation and human poetry, Allāh confirms that these words recited by Prophet Muḥammad ﷺ are not but a remembrance[157] and a Qur'ān[158] which is clear to all.

Āyah 70

لِيُنذِرَ مَن كَانَ حَيًّا وَيَحِقَّ الْقَوْلُ عَلَى الْكَافِرِينَ

To warn whoever is alive and establish the Word against the disbelievers

The Qur'ān has a dual purpose, which is stated directly here. First, it warns every living soul on the face of the earth, but only those whose hearts have life will benefit from the warning. And second, it serves as evidence by which those who reject belief will be condemned. Again, "the Word" refers to the decree of Allāh and His knowledge that a large portion of mankind is destined to be punished in Hell.[159] The justification for this decree and its suitability and necessity will become clear to all, for the Qur'ān will be proof of the fact that they were warned, even though they refused to heed the warning. Thus, it is both a mercy and a guidance for the believers and clear evidence against the disbelievers.

In this *āyah*, *kufr* (disbelief or rejection) is placed opposite to life, illustrating its similarity to physical death, where the faculties of hearing, sight and understanding do not function and are of no use at all. Thus, we know that in relation to the Qur'ān, there are two kinds of people – those who are alive and respond to it, and those who are dead and do not respond.

157Refer to *āyah* 11.

158A reference to this final scripture which literally means "a word construction, recital or reading."

159Refer to *āyah* 7.

Āyah 71

أَوَلَمْ يَرَوْا أَنَّا خَلَقْنَا لَهُم مِّمَّا عَمِلَتْ أَيْدِينَا أَنْعَامًا فَهُمْ لَهَا مَالِكُونَ

Do they not see that We have created for them from what Our hands have made, an'ām, and then they are their owners?

Next, Allāh (ﷻ) returns to the subject of His creation, which is placed at the disposal of mankind – this time with an example from animal life. *An'ām* cannot be literally translated as "cattle," but it is used to indicate camels, cows (or oxen), sheep and goats.[160] Or it can refer to camels specifically.

"Do they not see?" Al-Qurṭubī and Ibn Katheer have explained "sight" here as vision of the heart (i.e., "Do they not consider and contemplate and realize?") However, Sayyid Quṭb has chosen the more literal meaning: here is a sign from Allāh, visible to all, present before their eyes. These animals are created especially for man – for his benefit and enjoyment – yet they are creations from among the countless works of Allāh (ﷻ) produced by His hands.

"What is made by the hands of Allāh" has been defined by scholars as "that which He created Himself without partner or helper," i.e., His own creation. One must refrain from speculation about the nature of His hands and simply believe in all of what Allāh has said about Himself as being true in such capacity as is suitable to His absolute and perfect majesty. It is stated in the Qur'ān that Allāh has certain attributes such as hearing, sight, mercy, anger, etc. Yet He has disassociated Himself from the limitations of human attributes or human imagination. The correct *'aqeedah* (belief) concerning any descriptions of Allāh in the Qur'ān and in *ḥādīths* has been summarized thus by Ibn Taymiyyah: "Of the [true] belief in Allāh is belief in whatever He has described of Himself in His Book and whatever His Messenger has described of Him – [belief] free from distortion or suspension and free from qualification or comparison."[161]

These animals have been created for man, given to him and made subject to his use by ar-Raḥmān. "Ownership" refers to the temporary and partial ownership granted to man by Allāh, who is the actual owner of all things, including man himself. And it refers to the ability of an owner to control his possessions and do with them as he pleases.

---

[160]These are mentioned in *Sūrah al-An'ām,* 6:143-144.

[161]Distortion (*taḥreef*): Applying an allegorical meaning which will inevitably be incorrect since it is not based upon knowledge. Suspension (*ta'ṭeel*): Desertion of the concept altogether or denial that Allāh would have such an attribute or quality. Qualification (*takyeef*): Attempting to explain how a certain attribute or quality could be, while such knowledge lies only with Allāh. Comparison (*tamtheel*): Supposing that divine attributes resemble those of creation, while Allāh says: {لَيْسَ كَمِثْلِهِ شَيْءٌ} ***"There is nothing like unto Him."*** (*Sūrah ash-Shūrā,* 42:11.)

Āyah 72

وَذَلَّلْنَاهَا لَهُمْ فَمِنْهَا رَكُوبُهُمْ وَمِنْهَا يَأْكُلُونَ

And We have subjected these to them; so some they ride and some they eat.

Many animals have a wild and independent nature, but some have been created with a tame disposition and easily submit to man. They serve various purposes, two of which are mentioned here – transport and food. Other *āyahs* in the Qur'ān mention these and other uses:

الله الَّذِي جَعَلَ لَكُمُ الأَنعَامَ لِتَركَبُوا مِنهَا وَمِنهَا تَأكُلُونَ وَلَكُم فِيهَا مَنَافِعُ وَلِتَبلُغُوا عَلَيهَا حَاجَةً فِي صُدُورِكُم وَعَلَيهَا وَعَلَى الفُلكِ تُحمَلُونَ

"It is Allāh who made an'ām for you – some for you to ride and some for you to eat – for you in them are benefits, and that you may realize any need which is in your hearts; and upon them and upon ships you are carried."[162]

Said Qutādah describing the blessing in these animals, "Allāh has made them obedient and not of a refusing nature. Even if a small boy came to a camel, he could make it kneel, and if he wished, he could make it stand and drive it along, finding it submissive and willing to be led. In the same way, a train of one hundred or more camels could be led by the child, all following his direction." But if Allāh had not so willed, men could not have conquered and tamed such animals. As Sayyid Quṭb has pointed out, even a very small creature such as a fly cannot be forced to submit to man as long as Allāh has not created within it the tendency to compliance.

Āyah 73

وَلَهُمْ فِيهَا مَنَافِعُ وَمَشَارِبُ أَفَلَا يَشْكُرُونَ

And there are in them [various] benefits and drink. So will they not give thanks?

Ibn Katheer has mentioned some of the benefits alluded to in this *āyah*: "Camels are ridden, eaten and milked. Heavy burdens are carried by them on long journeys to distant lands. Cattle are eaten and milked and used to plow the earth. Sheep are eaten and milked. The hides, hair and wool of all are put to use..." Having once been the only means to fulfill basic needs, these animals and their byproducts are still essential to us, and it is difficult to imagine life without them. Meat and milk in particular are as yet indispensable to the well-being of man. *Sūrah an-Naḥl* gives a similar description (in *āyahs* five through seven), concluding:

---

[162]*Sūrah Ghāfir,* 40:79-80. See also *Sūrah al-Mu'minūn,* 23:21-22.

وَالْخَيْلَ وَالْبِغَالَ وَالْحَمِيرَ لِتَرْكَبُوهَا وَزِينَةً وَيَخْلُقُ مَا لاتَعلَمُونَ

"...And horses, mules and donkeys for you to ride and for beauty, and He creates that which you do not know."[163]

"So will they not give thanks?" If they could only appreciate such favors of which the Qur'ān reminds them, they would go on to realize that everything one uses during his lifetime upon earth is available only because of the care and mercy of the Creator. Their hearts would then be filled with gratitude and unceasing praise – the true thankfulness which is not limited to the tongue alone but is proved by obedience to Allāh in using His blessings in the manner acceptable to Him. For indeed, misuse of blessings, disobedience and the worship of others are the most shameful forms of ingratitude.

Āyah 74

وَاتَّخَذُوا مِن دُونِ اللهِ آلِهَةً لَعَلَّهُم يُنصَرُونَ

Yet they have taken for themselves gods other than Allāh that perhaps they would be helped.

Most men are ungrateful indeed. Turning away from the One who has provided all of the good things they enjoy, they attribute these blessings instead to the favor of certain deities or to other people, to blind fortune or to their own efforts. Acknowledging only immediate gratification, they rarely look beyond the life of this world.

Once there were idols of wood and stone. But those who bowed to them in fact worshipped the authority of custom and tradition – the authority of the tribe, family or society in which they sought security and well-being. *Shirk* (association) is still practiced in every corner of the earth, if not represented by pagan idols, then by numerous other obsessions to which the adherents of non-Islāmic culture devote themselves – wealth and status, popular personalities, current ideologies, political parties, personal achievements, etc... وَمِنَ النَّاسِ مَن يَتَّخِذُ مِن دُونِ اللهِ أَندَادًا يُحِبُّونَهُم كَحُبِّ اللهِ ***"And among the people are those who take other than Allāh as equals [to Him]. They love them as they [should] love Allāh."***[164] Moreover, *shirk* is represented by the people's belief in and dependence upon these earthly powers rather than upon the power of Allāh, even though they might bow to Him superficially in prayer. Association takes many forms and varies with time and place: Allāh confirms in the Qur'ān: وَمَا يُؤمِنُ أَكثَرُهُم بِاللهِ إلا وَهُم مُشرِكُونَ ***"And most of them believe not in Allāh except that they associate [others with Him]."***[165]

---

[163]Sūrah an-Naḥl, 16:8.
[164]Sūrah al-Baqarah, 2:165.
[165]Sūrah Yūsuf, 12:106.

Āyah 75

لايَستَطِيعُونَ نَصرَهُم وَهُم لَهُم جُندٌ مُحضَرُونَ

They are not able to help them, and, [moreover], they are soldiers in attendance for them.

Can dependence upon creation be compared to dependence upon the Creator? Even if Shayṭān should make it seem fruitful for a time on the earth, the worship of false gods can only lead to ruin. Placing trust and hope in them brings disappointment in worldly life and even greater loss in the Hereafter:

أَم لَهُم آلِهَةٌ تَمنَعُهُم مِن دُونِنَا. لايَستَطِيعُونَ نَصرَ أَنفُسِهِم وَلاهُم مِنَّا يُصحَبُونَ

"Or have they gods that defend them other than Us? They are not able to help [even] themselves, nor can they be protected from Us."[166]

مَثَلُ الَّذِينَ اتَّخَذُوا مِن دُونِ اللهِ أَولِيَاءَ كَمَثَلِ العَنكَبُوتِ اتَّخَذَت بَيتًا وَإِنَّ أَوهَنَ البُيُوتِ لَبَيتُ العَنكَبُوتِ لَو كَانُوا يَعلَمُونَ

"The example of those who take protectors other than Allāh is like that of the spider who takes for itself a home. And truly the weakest of homes is the home of the spider, if they only knew."[167]

While Allāh continues eternally to sustain and reign over all creation whether or not His creatures recognize Him, those gods created by men must be maintained and protected by their worshippers in order to exist. If one is amused by the thought of soldiers being posted to protect stone idols from harm in ancient times, he should contemplate the fact that the tyrants and oppressors of our own age who set themselves up as gods to be praised and obeyed without question are just as vulnerable. Their servants must continually stand guard to protect them from those of their people who refuse submission, using all means of propaganda, bribery, threat and persecution to keep their lords in power. Yet can these slaves expect help from their masters when problems arise, or are they merely cast aside as unworthy, insignificant and dispensable after their years of devoted service?

In addition to the aforementioned explanation of this *āyah,* a second interpretation has been given, which is as follows: If any man thinks that he can be helped by lords other than Allāh, his trust will betray him on the Day of Judgement. Those he had obeyed and worshipped will be brought forward as soldiers set against him in Hellfire, cursing him and disassociating themselves from him. And Allāh knows best.

---

[166]Sūrah al-Anbiyā', 21:43.
[167]Sūrah al-'Ankabūt, 29:41.

❧ ❧ Āyah 76 ☙ ☙

فَلا يَحزُنْكَ قَولُهُم. إنَّا نَعلَمُ مَا يُسِرُّونَ وَمَا يُعلِنُونَ

So let not their speech grieve you. Indeed We know what they conceal and what they declare.

Allāh (ﷻ) addresses His messenger with words of comfort and assurance: "Do not be saddened by the campaign of those who waste themselves in the worship of creation, O Muḥammad, against you. And do not be saddened by their denunciation of you as a poet, magician or madman or by their denial of your message to them." For those who give loyalty to others and refuse gratitude to Allāh cannot conceal themselves from His knowledge. He is well aware of their innermost secrets, as well as their public declarations. He knows that deep in their hearts they are not convinced of what they say (as Abū Jahl admitted privately to al-Akhnas bin Shurayq), but they will not relent in their struggle to preserve their own status and authority.

❧ ❧ Āyah 77 ☙ ☙

أَوَلَم يَرَ الإِنسَانُ أَنَّا خَلَقنَاهُ مِن نُطفَةٍ فَإِذَا هُوَ خَصِيمٌ مُبِينٌ

Does mankind not consider that We created him from a sperm-drop – then he has become a clear adversary?

The *sūrah* concludes with a discussion of resurrection, the concept most often denied by disbelievers. Evidence is now presented in a final statement which leaves no room for further argument. The circumstance of this revelation was described by several of the *tābi'een* as follows: One of the influential leaders of the Quraysh, Ubayy bin Khalaf,[168] came to the Messenger of Allāh ﷺ with a decayed bone in hand. While crumbling it and scattering it in the wind, he taunted, "O Muḥammad, do you claim that Allāh will bring this to life?" He ﷺ replied, "Yes. Allāh will cause you to die, then He will bring you to life, and then He will pack you into the Fire." Immediately thereafter Allāh revealed the last *āyahs* of *Sūrah Yā Seen.* After quoting this incident Ibn Katheer has pointed out that the *āyahs* are general in answer to everyone who denies resurrection, as the word "mankind" (*al-insān*) indicates.

Elsewhere in the Qur'ān, Allāh reminds the proud human race of its humble origin:

أَلَم نَخلُقكُم مِن مَاءٍ مَهِينٍ

"Did We not create you from a liquid disdained?"[169]

---

[168]Some said it was al-'Aaس bin Wā'il. It is possible that more than one person came to the Prophet (ﷺ) with the same objection.
[169]Sūrah al-Mursalāt, 77:20.

Upon the creation of Ādam from the earth's dust, Allāh willed that his descendants would enter the world through the same reproductive process as the basest of animals – a fact which man in his delusion of intellect and self-importance would often prefer to ignore. Yet the reality stands that he evolved from a tiny cell in a drop of fluid belittled in his own estimation. It is related that the Messenger of Allāh ﷺ one day spat into the palm of his hand and put his finger into it, saying, "Allāh *ta'ālā* says, 'O son of Ādam, how can you consider [anything] impossible for Me when I have created you from the likes of this?' "[170]

The process of development from sperm cell to fetus to child to man is in itself a sign of Allāh's creative power.[171] With no contrivance on his part, the human being grows physically and mentally until he becomes aware of himself as an individual and of certain characteristics and skills he has been given. But the disbeliever attributes these gifts to himself only and considers that he is self-sufficient. When reminded of his true position as a servant of Allāh, his pride will not allow him to reconsider. Upon being warned of the account and judgement in a life to come, his reaction is denial and rejection. He becomes an open adversary to those who warn him and ultimately to Allāh Himself. The Qur'ān omits the time factor in this *āyah,* showing clearly the absurdity of a creature who, emerging from a lowly drop of semen, has the audacity to stand up in antagonism against his all-powerful Creator.

Āyah 78

وَضَرَبَ لَنَا مَثَلاً وَنَسِيَ خَلْقَهُ قَالَ مَن يُحْيِي الْعِظَامَ وَهِيَ رَمِيمٌ

He presents an example for Us and forgets his [own] creation. He says, "Who will give life to bones when they are decayed?"

"The son of Ādam insults Me and he should not insult Me, and he denies Me and he should not deny Me. His insult is his saying that I have a son. As for his denial of Me, it is when he says, 'He will not recreate me as He originated me.' " This statement of Allāh (*subḥānahu wa ta'ālā*) is recorded in a *ḥadīth qudsī.*[172] Unable to imagine anything beyond human power or beyond the reach of their own senses, the arrogant and short-sighted, in scoffing at the concept of resurrection, compare the Creator to creation, with all its limitations. They offer an example by which they think they can prove the finality of death – the last, visible remains of a body disintegrating into dust, soon to disappear

[170]Portion of a *ḥadīth* narrated by Aḥmad and Ibn Mājah.
[171]See Sayyid Quṭb's *tafseer* of *Sūrah aṭ-Ṭāriq,* 86:8 (*In the Shade of the Qur'ān,* vol. 30) for an excellent description.
[172]Al-Bukhārī.

completely. Who could ever restore this to life?[173] But they have forgotten how their own creation began – from dust and then from a single cell. They have forgotten that they were created by a power beyond their own, without their presence or their consent, from nothing. مَا أَشْهَدتُّهُمْ خَلْقَ السَّمَاوَاتِ وَالأَرْضِ وَلا خَلْقَ أَنفُسِهِمْ ***"I did not show them the creation of the heavens and the earth nor the creation of themselves."***[174]

Referring directly to the challenge by the Qurayshī chiefs, the Qur'ān repeats their expression of ridicule, attracting the attention of all for the answer to come. For the question put to the Prophet ﷺ, with all its intended sarcasm and insolence, is to serve as a base for the following discourse in which the final evidence is put forth.

Āyah 79

قُل يُحْيِيهَا الَّذِي أَنشَأَهَا أَوَّلَ مَرَّةٍ وَهُوَ بِكُلِّ خَلْقٍ عَلِيمٌ

Say, "He will give them life – who produced them the first time – and He is of all creation supreme in knowledge"

The Prophet ﷺ had given an appropriate answer to the rudeness of Ubayy bin Khalaf and others. But Allāh (*subḥānahu wa ta'ālā*) ordered him to give an answer to the doubters and questioners of every age. He commanded him ﷺ to give the answer obvious to any who would reflect upon the state of the universe – that the bones as a part of the human body will be created and brought to life once more by the same power which created them in the first place without precedent, from nothing at all. For He who is able to originate creation at will can certainly renew it at will. This point is also emphasized in other *āyahs*:

وَيَقُولُ الإِنسَانُ أَإِذَا مَا مِتُّ لَسَوفَ أُخرَجُ حَيًّا أَوَلا يَذكُرُ الإِنسَانُ أَنَّا خَلَقنَاهُ مِن قَبلُ وَلَم يَكُ شَيئًا

"And man says, 'When I have died, will I indeed be brought forth alive?' Then does man not remember that We created him before, while he was nothing?"[175]

أَفَعَيِينَا بِالخَلقِ الأَوَّلِ بَل هُم فِي لَبْسٍ مِن خَلقٍ جَدِيدٍ

"Did We fail in the first creation? Yet they are in doubt of a new creation."[176]

أَفَرَأَيتُم مَا تُمنُونَ أَأَنتُم تَخلُقُونَهُ أَم نَحنُ الخَالِقُونَ نَحنُ قَدَّرنَا بَينَكُمُ المَوتَ وما نحن بمسبوقين عَلَى أَن نُبَدِّلَ أَمثَالَكُم وَنُنشِئَكُم فِي مَا لاتَعلَمُونَ وَلَقَد عَلِمتُمُ النَّشأَةَ الأُولَى فَلَو لاتَذَكَّرُونَ

"Do you see that which you ejaculate? Is it you who creates it, or are We the Creator?

---

[173]See similar *āyahs* – 17:48-49, 23:35-36, 23:82-83, 27:67, 37:16-17, 50:3, 56:47-48 and 79:10-11.
[174]Sūrah al-Kahf, 18:51.
[175]Sūrah Maryam, 19:66-67.
[176]Sūrah Qāf, 50:15.

We have decreed death among you, and We are not to be defeated in that We shall change your kind and create you in that which you do not know. And you have already known the first creation, so will you not remember?" 177

In *Sūrah al-'Ankabūt* Allāh tells His Messenger ﷺ to direct man towards the observation and study that will lead him to this very conclusion:

قُلْ سِيرُوا فِي الأَرْضِ فَانْظُرُوا كَيفَ بَدَأَ الخَلْقَ ثُمَّ اللهُ يُنشِئُ النَّشأَةَ الآخِرَةَ

"Say, 'Proceed throughout the earth and observe how He began creation. Then Allāh will bring up the final creation.'" 178

Man is a product of the earth.179 His close association with it in life and death provides him with ample opportunities for examination and contemplation. He is invited to look into the beginnings of life upon the earth – plant, animal and human – in every place and from every angle, for here before him are visible examples of the continuing creative process.

يخرِجُ الحَيَّ مِنَ المَيِّتِ وَيُخرِجُ المَيِّتَ مِنَ الحَيِّ وَيُحيِي الأَرضَ بَعدَ مَوتِهَا وَكَذَلِكَ تُخرَجُونَ

"He extracts the living from the dead, and He extracts the dead from the living; and He gives life to the earth after it was lifeless. And thus will you be extracted." *180*

One might look into the birth of an atom or a galaxy as well, for all creation reflects the power of He who has promised to recreate: كَمَا بَدَأنَا أَوَّلَ خَلقٍ نُعِيدُهُ وَعدًا عَلَينَا إِنَّا كُنَّا فَاعِلِينَ

"As We began the first creation, We shall repeat it. [That is] a promise binding upon Us. Assuredly We shall carry it out." *181*

"And He is of all creation supreme in knowledge." Indeed, Allāh (ﷻ) knows its every aspect, its whereabouts, its future, its final destination.

Āyah 80

الَّذِي جَعَلَ لَكُم مِنَ الشَّجَرِ الأَخضَرِ نَارًا فَإِذَا أَنتُم مِنهُ تُوقِدُونَ

The One who made for you from the green tree, fire, and then you ignite from it

A specific example is given in this *āyah* to show the unlimited nature of creative

---

177*Sūrah al-Wāqi'ah,* 56:58-62. An alternative meaning has been given for *āyah* 61: "That We shall replace the likes of you [with others upon the earth] and create you [in the Hereafter] in that which you do not know."

178Sūrah al-'Ankabūt, 29:20.

179As shown in 7:25, 20:55 and similar *āyahs,* such as *Sūrah Nūḥ,* 71:17-18, which states: وَاللهُ أَنبَتَكُم مِنَ الأَرضِ نَبَاتًا ثُمَّ يُعِيدُكُم فِيهَا وَيُخرِجُكُم إِخرَاجًا ***"And Allāh has caused you to grow from the earth. Then He will return you to it and [again] extract you."***

180i.e., on the Day of Judgement. *Sūrah ar-Rūm,* 30:19.

181Sūrah al-Anbiyā', 21:104.

power and that realities are not confined to appearances or expectations. To produce an element from its opposite is a greater wonder than that of systematic development, although it is easily within the ability of Allāh.[182]

The tree could not sprout, grow or remain green without absorbing and retaining large quantities of water, the very element which extinguishes fire. Yet fire is produced by the friction of two green twigs against each other – fire which in turn burns green trees. This phenomenon has been explained in recent years by the fact that solar energy is absorbed by leaves, stored in branches and then released upon agitation or ignition. One type of tree known by the desert Arabs was leafless but nonetheless would sometimes ignite itself during a wind. Praise be to Him who has given all things their particular properties and characteristics!

❧ ❧ Āyah 81 ❧ ❧

أَوَلَيْسَ الَّذِي خَلَقَ السَّمَاوَاتِ وَالأَرْضَ بِقَادِرٍ عَلَى أَن يَخْلُقَ مِثْلَهُم بَلَى وَهُوَ الخَلَّاقُ العَلِيمُ

Is not He who created the heavens and the earth able to create the likes of them? Yes, [it is so]. And He is the omniscient Creator.

The creation of the heavens and the earth is so tremendous as to impose failure on human imagination. Within the created universe, processes of formation, transformation, disintegration and reformation constantly occur and reoccur – creation giving way to creation, matter to energy, energy to matter, life to death, death to life. None of this is difficult for Allāh, who poses the question of this verse. Is He not able, after creating all of this from non-existence, to reconstruct the bodies of those souls who await judgement? As stated in another *āyah*:

أَوَلَمْ يَرَوْا أَنَّ اللهَ الَّذِي خَلَقَ السَّمَاوَاتِ وَالأَرْضَ وَلَمْ يَعْيَ بِخَلْقِهِنَّ بِقَادِرٍ عَلَى أَن يُحْيِيَ المَوْتَى

"Do they not see that Allāh, who created the heavens and earth and was not incapable of their creation, is able to give life to the dead?"[183]

Commentators have pointed out that all creation is accomplished with equal facility by Allāh. However, for the purpose of clarification, a parallel is drawn from human experience. In doing something for the second time, a man is no longer hindered by the same degree of unfamiliarity. Repetition requires less thought and effort on his part; therefore, the task becomes easier for him than it was previously. Allāh alludes to this in the Qur'ān:

---

[182]Another reference to this phenomenon is found in *Sūrah al-Wāqi'ah,* 56:71-72.
[183]Sūrah al-Aḥqāf, 46:33.

أَوَلَم يَرَوا كَيفَ يُبدِئُ الله الخَلقَ ثُمَّ يُعِيدُهُ إِنَّ ذَلِكَ عَلَى اللهِ يَسِيرٌ

"Have they not considered how Allāh begins creation [and] then He repeats it? Certainly that is simple for Allāh."[184]

وَهُوَ الَّذِي يَبدَئُ الخَلقَ ثُمَّ يُعِيدُهُ وَهُوَ أَهوَنُ عَلَيهِ

"And it is He who begins creation, then repeats it, and that is [even] easier for Him."[185]

Origination or repetition – all is easy for Allāh. The material of creation is already in existence, merely to be developed at His command. And what is the creation of man in comparison to that of the heavens and the earth and all they contain?[186]

زَعَمَ الَّذِينَ كَفَرُوا أَن لَن يُبعَثُوا قُل بَلَى وَرَبِّي لَتُبعَثُنَّ ثُمَّ لَتُنَبَّؤُنَّ بِمَا عَمِلتُم وَذَلِكَ عَلَى اللهِ يَسِيرٌ

"The disbelievers claim that they will never be resurrected. Say, 'Yes, [on the contrary], by my Lord. You shall certainly be resurrected; then you will be informed of what you have done. And that is easy for Allāh.' "[187]

Āyah 82

إِنَّمَا أَمرُهُ إِذَا أَرَادَ شَيئًا أَن يَقُولَ لَهُ كُنْ فَيَكُونُ

His command when He intends a thing is only that He says to it, "Be" and it is.

How creation is effected has been expressed by Allāh simply as a direction given by Him in one word: "Be."[188] Reliable scholars have given very little commentary on this and similar *āyahs* in which existence comes about by decree of the Creator, except for the confirmation that when Allāh says to a thing, "Be," then nothing can prevent, oppose or delay its being. As stated in *Sūrah al-Qamar*: وَمَا أَمْرُنَا إِلا وَاحِدَةٌ كَلَمحٍ بِالبَصَرِ ***"And Our command is but once like a glance of the eye."***[189] Whether through physical laws of the universe which He has ordained or by miracle outside the normal course of events, the primal cause of all that has been and ever will be is Allāh's command. He but says to it, "Be" and it is.

---

[184]Sūrah al-'Ankabūt, 29:19.

[185]Sūrah ar-Rūm, 30:27.

[186]Allāh confirms: لَخَلقُ السَّمَاوَاتِ وَالأَرضِ أَكبَرُ مِن خَلقِ النَّاسِ وَلَكِنَّ أَكثَرَ النَّاسِ لايَعلَمُونَ **"Indeed, the creation of the heavens and the earth is greater than the creation of people, but most of the people know not."** (Sūrah Ghāfir, 40:57.)

[187]Sūrah at-Taghābun, 64:7.

[188]Belief in Allāh's words or speech is again subject to the conditions mentioned by Ibn Taymiyyah. Refer to *āyah* 71.

[189]Sūrah al-Qamar, 54:50.

Āyah 83

فَسُبْحَانَ الَّذِي بِيَدِهِ مَلَكُوتُ كُلِّ شَيْءٍ وَإِلَيْهِ تُرْجَعُونَ

So praise be to Him in whose hand is the dominion of all things, and to Him you will be returned.

Praise – a suitable closing to a *sūrah* which has taken us beyond the limits of time and space, into the human soul, and through various aspects of creation – calling us to witness the signs of Allāh. Praise – which is due to Him absolutely, by reason of His attributes of unity and perfection and by reason of the debt of all existence to its Creator. The precise meaning of "*subḥāna*" is more than "praise," as such. It is a declaration that Allāh is far removed from any lack, failing or imperfection that might be attributed to Him by man and free from any equal or associate.

"Dominion" refers to sovereignty and possession, to right and power, to absolute ownership, authority and control over everything in existence, whether visible or invisible. And as is expressed in a similar *āyah*:

تَبَارَكَ الَّذِي بِيَدِهِ الْمُلْكُ

"Blessed is He in whose hand is dominion."[190]

All creation is in the hand of Allāh – that which has been and that which is yet to be.

Praise, then, is due to Him and Him alone, the Eternal, the Absolute, who holds destiny in His hand and to whom every soul shall be returned.

والحمد لله رب العالمين

---

[190] Sūrah al-Mulk, 67:1.

Lightning Source UK Ltd.
Milton Keynes UK
UKHW010907080223
416610UK00013B/743